This book belongs to

....

Grandma's
Special Recipes

Slow Cooking

hinkler

Published by Hinkler Books Pty Ltd
45–55 Fairchild Street
Heatherton Victoria 3202 Australia
www.hinkler.com.au

hinkler

Text and images © Anthony Carroll 2010
Design © Hinkler Books Pty Ltd 2013

Cover design: Beverley Gutierrez and Hinkler Design Studio
Stitching, embroidery and screen-printed illustrations created by Beverley Gutierrez
Internal design: Beverley Gutierrez and Hinkler Design Studio
Typesetting: MPS Limited
Prepress: Graphic Print Group

ISBN: 978 1 7435 2040 6

Printed and bound in China

Contents

The slow cooker

In earlier years, the stockpot was perfect for corned and pickled meats, ideal for soups and casseroles and superb for stewed fruits, as it happily bubbled in the hearth during those cold wintry months. However, that was the limit of its usefulness. Now that you are the owner of a new electric version, you will find that there are a great number of dishes that you had never thought could be cooked so well and with so little difficulty.

Having a slow cooker is like having a genie at home, cooking while you are away. When you arrive home, delicious food is waiting and there is no preparation mess to clean up. All of this was done the night before or earlier in the day. Having a slow cooker adds a note of serenity in the kitchen. You are free to relax for a few minutes, and there is even time for a glass of wine. You do not need to rush, dinner awaits without fear of drying out or overcooking.

Another feature of the slow cooker is that it is also a marvellous food warmer and server. It is excellent for buffets and pot-luck dinner parties. The low temperature setting allows you to keep previously cooked food warm so guests can help themselves. It is ideal for heat-and-serve dishes.

Because the slow cooking concept calls for long cooking, it forces you to organise in advance. It means you get set for dinner early in the day rather than relying on something fast in the evening. You can even perform some of the necessary preparation, such as cutting up the meat, peeling the vegetables and organising all the other ingredients, the evening before.

Putting the recipe together the next morning takes only a few minutes, when all the pre-organising is done.

Slow cooking, made possible by low temperature, is the key to fine flavour, juiciness and lack of shrinkage, especially with meat and poultry. Food cooked at low temperature also retains more minerals and vitamins in the food. Low temperature is below 200°C (400°F) and high is around 300°C (570°F).

The wrap-around heating method makes cooking in this way possible. It eliminates all of the heat concentrating on the bottom of the cooker that will generally cause scorching and will require you to spend some time stirring when the food starts to stick.

When the cooker is turned to high, you will find that this temperature is not hot enough to brown the meat. We believe it is best to brown meat in a frying pan or in the oven prior to placing it into the slow cooker. This will enhance the flavour of your dish. You will get an even better result if you deglaze the frying pan or roasting dish with a little stock or wine then add this to your cooker.

One drawback with slow cooking is the reduction in colour of brightly coloured vegetables, especially peas and beans. A way of keeping the colour constant is to only put them into your slow cooker as a last-minute inclusion.

If you try experimenting with the recipes in this book, you will find the results will astound you. Your real problem will be selecting which recipe to try next, as all of our offerings are easy to assemble with local ingredients, almost cook themselves, and offer a real taste sensation.

Our chefs and kitchen staff explored the potential of slow cooking by testing hundreds of recipes, the success ratio was very high indeed. Our real problem was selecting which recipes to leave out of the book.

After creating recipes to suit the appliance and cooking method and nursing them through the testing stages to finished product, it was hard to part with any of them. However, there is compensation in knowing that what did make the final selection is the best of its type: casseroles, curries, soups, desserts, meats, fish, poultry and vegetarian dishes.

You will find that in addition to all the foods you know can be cooked with success in your slow cooker, there is a great range of recipes you may not have thought of previously, such as meatloaves, puddings, breads and cakes.

You will find that cooking times vary considerably, even when cooking a recipe a second time. Times depend so much on the tenderness and texture of the particular food being cooked.

You will find that these recipes represent the tip of the iceberg in relation to the variety that can be cooked successfully in your slow cooker. Follow the basic instructions in this book and you will find that you can adapt literally hundreds of your own recipes for slow cooking.

Cleaning and caring for your slow cooker

- Never submerge the appliance in water. Remove the cooking bowl and place it in the dishwasher or wash with hot soapy water as soon as you empty it. Do not pour in cold water if the bowl is still hot from cooking.

- Do not use abrasive cleaning compounds. A cloth, sponge or rubber spatula will usually remove the residue – if necessary a plastic cleaning pad may be used.

- To remove water spots and other stains, use a non-abrasive cleaner or vinegar, and wipe with olive oil to restore the sparkle.

- The metal liner may be cleaned with a damp cloth or scouring pad, or sprayed lightly with all-purpose cleaner to maintain its original sheen.

- The outside of the appliance may be cleaned with a soft cloth and warm soapy water and wiped dry. Do not use abrasive cleaners on the outside.

- Care should be taken in not bumping the ceramic insert with metal spoons or water taps. A sharp knock can break or chip the bowl.

- Do not put frozen or very cold foods in the slow cooker if the appliance has been pre-heated or is hot to the touch.

Safety hints for your slow cooker

When using electrical appliances, basic safety precautions should always be followed, including the following:

- Read all instructions and become thoroughly familiar with the unit.

- Do not touch hot surfaces – always use handles or knobs.

- To protect against electrical hazards, do not immerse cord, plugs or cooking unit in water or other liquid.

- Close supervision is necessary when appliance is in use or near children.

- Unplug from outlet when not in use, before putting on or taking off parts, and before cleaning.

- Do not operate an appliance with a damaged cord or plug or after the appliance malfunctions or has been damaged in any manner. Return appliance to nearest authorised service facility for examination, repair or adjustment.

- The use of accessory attachments not recommended by the manufacturer may cause a hazard.

- Do not use outdoors or on a wet surface.

- Do not let the cord hang over the edge of the counter or table, or touch hot surfaces.

- Do not place slow cooker units on or near a hot gas or electric burner, or in a heated oven.

- Extreme caution must be used when moving the appliance containing hot oil or other liquids.

- Always attach to appliance first, then plug cord into the wall outlet. To disconnect, turn any control to off, then remove the plug from the wall outlet.

- Do not use the appliance for anything other than its intended use.

Soups

To feel safe and warm on a cold wet night, all you really need is soup.

Laurie Colwin (1944–1992)

Dinner Party Beef Consommé

Preparation time: 20 minutes
Cooking time: 8 hours
Serves: 2–3

60g (2oz) butter
1 white onion, finely sliced
400g (14oz) canned beef consommé
1 small carrot, julienned
½ stalk celery, sliced thinly on the diagonal
½ small parsnip, julienned
salt and seasoned pepper blend
2 teaspoons brandy
¼ cup parsley or chives, chopped, to garnish

1   In a frying pan (skillet), melt the butter and sauté the onion until soft.

2   Add onion to slow cooker with 1 cup water and all remaining ingredients except
    brandy and parsley or chives. Simmer for 8 hours on low, ready for serving at dinner.

3   Add brandy and serve garnished with parsley or chives.

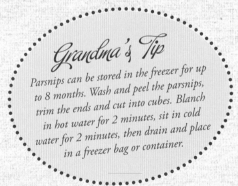

Grandma's Tip

Parsnips can be stored in the freezer for up
to 8 months. Wash and peel the parsnips,
trim the ends and cut into cubes. Blanch
in hot water for 2 minutes, sit in cold
water for 2 minutes, then drain and place
in a freezer bag or container.

Lamb Shank Broth

Preparation time: 20 minutes
Cooking time: 16 hours
Serves: 6

2 lamb shanks
salt and freshly ground black pepper
1 carrot, diced
1 parsnip, diced
2 stalks celery, sliced
½ turnip, diced
1 white onion, diced
½ cup barley
60g (2oz) chopped parsley, plus extra to garnish

1 Place lamb shanks in slow cooker and cover with water almost to the top of the
   cooker. Add salt and pepper and simmer overnight on low. Allow to cool, then skim
   off the fat.

2 Remove the shanks, which should be very tender, and chop the meat. Return meat
   to stock (broth) with all other ingredients and simmer for at least 8 hours on low
   (or much longer if desired). Serve very hot, sprinkled with a little extra fresh parsley.

Grandma's Note

Pearl barley is the most common
form of barley. It is less chewy than
hulled barley but also less nutritious
because the outer bran layer has
been removed.

Chicken and Oat Soup

Preparation time: 30 minutes
Cooking time: 16 hours
Serves: 10

1.5kg (3lb) chicken, whole
2 chicken stock cubes (bouillon)
2 carrots, diced
1 parsnip, diced
2 onions, diced
2 stalks celery, sliced
120g (4oz) rolled oats (coarse oatmeal)
¼ cup commercial soup mix
salt and freshly ground black pepper
¼ cup parsley, chopped, plus extra to garnish

1 Place the chicken in the slow cooker, cover with water and add crumbled stock cubes
   (bouillon). Cook on low overnight. The next day, remove the chicken from the stock
   and allow stock to cool. Skim off fat.

2 Remove breast meat from the chicken, chop finely and put aside. The remainder of
   chicken meat may be used in sandwiches, chicken croquettes, chicken loaf, and so on.

3 Add all remaining ingredients to the stock in the slow cooker. Simmer on low for
   at least 8 hours or overnight, adding the chicken breast meat during the last hour.
   Adjust seasoning if necessary, and serve with a sprinkling of extra parsley in each bowl.

Minestrone

Preparation time: 25 minutes
Cooking time: 10 hours
Serves: 6–8

1 veal shank, trimmed of fat
1 clove garlic, crushed
1 medium carrot, finely chopped
1 large onion, chopped
2 cups beef stock (broth)
1 teaspoon salt
1 teaspoon freshly ground black pepper
3 cups tomato juice
3 tomatoes, chopped
2 teaspoons yeast extract
2 bay leaves
1 sprig thyme
½ cup parsley, chopped
½ cup macaroni
60g (2oz) cabbage, shredded
parmesan cheese, grated, to garnish

1 Combine all ingredients (except cheese) in the slow cooker. Simmer for at least
   10 hours on low.

2 Remove shank from soup once meat is falling from bone, and chop coarsely. Replace
   meat in slow cooker and cook on high until thoroughly reheated. Taste the soup, and
   if the tomatoes have made it 'sharp', add a little raw sugar. Garnish with parmesan
   cheese and serve with crusty bread.

Creamy Pumpkin Soup

Preparation time: 25 minutes
Cooking time: 3–6 hours
Serves: 6–8

500g (1lb) bright yellow pumpkin, peeled and cut into chunks
2 cups tomato juice
1 tablespoon raw sugar
2 chicken stock cubes (bouillon), crumbled
dash of hot chilli (pepper) sauce
1 bay leaf
salt and freshly ground black pepper
½ cup thickened (whipping) cream
¼ cup parsley, chopped

1 Combine all ingredients except cream and parsley in slow cooker with 8 cups of water. Cook until pumpkin is tender, approximately 4–5 hours on low or 3 hours on high.

2 Remove bay leaf and process the mixture, a cupful at a time, in a blender or food processor. Return mixture to slow cooker and reheat. About 1 hour before serving, add cream and allow to heat through. Serve sprinkled with fresh parsley.

Grandma's Tip

For a milder flavour, replace the chilli (pepper) sauce with tomato sauce (ketchup) mixed with small amounts of vinegar, brown sugar and spices such as cinnamon and cloves.

Tomato, Lentil and Basil Soup

Preparation time: 40 minutes
Cooking time: 3 hours
Serves: 4

½ cup brown lentils
1kg (2lb) Roma tomatoes
2 onions, diced
2 tablespoons tomato paste (purée)
3 cups vegetable stock (broth)
1 bay leaf
freshly ground black pepper
½ cup fresh basil, chopped, plus extra leaves for garnish

1   Rinse the lentils, drain and add them to a large saucepan of boiling water. Simmer, covered, for 25 minutes or until tender, then drain, rinse and set aside.

2   Meanwhile, place the tomatoes in a bowl, cover with boiling water and leave for 30 seconds, then drain. Remove the skins, deseed and chop.

3   In a slow cooker on high, add the onions and stir in the tomatoes, tomato purée, stock (broth), bay leaf and pepper. Cover and simmer for 2¼ hours.

4   Remove and discard the bay leaf, then purée the soup until smooth in a food processor or with a hand-held blender. Stir in the lentils and chopped basil, then reheat on high. Serve garnished with the fresh basil leaves.

Roasted Red Vegetable and Bread Soup

Preparation time: 30 minutes
Cooking time: 2 hours 30 minutes
Serves: 4

2 tablespoons olive oil
1kg (2lb) Roma tomatoes
2 red capsicums (peppers)
3 cloves garlic, crushed
2 onions, finely diced
2 teaspoons ground cumin
1 teaspoon ground coriander
4 cups chicken stock (broth)
2 slices white bread, crusts removed and torn into pieces
1 tablespoon balsamic vinegar
salt and freshly ground black pepper

1 Preheat oven to 180°C (350°F). Lightly oil a baking dish, place tomatoes and capsicums
   (peppers) in the dish and bake for 20 minutes or until the skins have blistered. Add in
   the garlic, onion, cumin and coriander for the last 5 minutes. Set aside to cool, then take
   out the tomatoes and capsicums (peppers), remove their skins and roughly chop.

2 Set slow cooker on high, add the cooked vegetables and stock (broth) and cook for
   2 hours. Add bread, balsamic vinegar and salt and pepper, and cook for a further
   50 minutes.

Pea and Ham Soup

Preparation time: 20 minutes
Cooking time: 8–12 hours
Serves: 6–8

1½ cups yellow or green dried peas
1 onion, diced
2 bay leaves
1 sprig thyme
salt and freshly ground black pepper
1 medium smoked ham hock
8 cups chicken or vegetable stock (broth)

1   Rinse peas and place in slow cooker. Add all remaining ingredients to slow cooker
    and cook on low for at least 8 hours. This soup improves with long, slow cooking,
    so 10–12 hours will enhance the flavour.

2   Remove bay leaves, thyme and ham hock. Cut the fat off the hock, chop the meat and
    replace it in the soup. Serve very hot.

Grandma's Note

Dried peas are a good source of fibre. They are also packed with protein, vitamins and minerals, and are low in fat.

Scallop Chowder

Preparation time: 10 minutes
Cooking time: 2–3 hours
Serves: 4–6

12 scallops, diced
½ cup white wine
1 sprig thyme
1 bay leaf
1 cup thickened (whipping) cream
12 cups milk
2 cups chicken stock (broth)
salt and freshly ground black pepper
6 spring (green) onions, chopped

1 Place scallops into slow cooker with white wine and herbs and cook on low
   for 1 hour.

2 Combine remaining ingredients and add to slow cooker. Cook on high for
   1–1½ hours or on low for 1½–2 hours until heated through, but do not overcook.

Grandma's Note

People who don't like other types of seafood often enjoy scallops because scallops are mild, sweet and soft. Scallops are also a good source of protein and are very high in vitamin B12.

Beef

I am a great eater of beef, and I believe that does harm to my wit.

William Shakespeare (1564–1616)

Basic Beef Casserole

Preparation time: 25 minutes
Cooking time: 6–8 hours
Serves: 4–5

1 tablespoon vegetable oil
1kg (2lb) blade steak, trimmed and cubed
2 onions, chopped
2 beef stock cubes (bouillon), crumbled
2 carrots, sliced
1 parsnip, sliced
salt and freshly ground black pepper
1 bouquet garni
30g (1oz) butter
2 tablespoons plain (all-purpose) flour

1 Heat the oil in a frying pan (skillet). Pat steak cubes dry with absorbent paper and
   brown them on all sides.

2 Add onion to pan and sauté until softened. Mix stock cubes (bouillon) in 1 cup
   hot water.

3 Place stock, meat, onion, carrots, parsnip, salt and pepper, and bouquet garni in
   slow cooker. Cook for approximately 7–8 hours on low or 6–7 hours on high. Remove
   bouquet garni. Blend butter and flour together thoroughly and stir into hot casserole
   a dab at a time to thicken. Serve with rice and garnish with chopped parsley.

Grandma's Note

A bouquet garni is a bundle of fresh herbs tied together. The herbs usually include parsley, thyme and bay leaves. The herbs can be tied with string or wrapped in cheesecloth to stop them from breaking up during cooking.

Beef and Vegetable Casserole

Preparation time: 30 minutes
Cooking time: 4–8 hours
Serves: 4

500g (1lb) blade steak, trimmed and cubed
2 white onions, thinly sliced
425g (15oz) canned Roma tomatoes
1 beef stock cube (bouillon), crumbled
½ clove garlic, crushed
½ teaspoon dried marjoram
¼ cup parsley, chopped
salt and freshly ground black pepper
250g (8oz) zucchini (courgette), sliced

1   Place beef and onion in slow cooker. Add the tomatoes, reserving ¼ cup juice, mix the stock cube (bouillon) into the juice, then add to cooker with the garlic, marjoram and half the parsley. Season to taste.

2   Cook on low for 6–8 hours or on high 4–5 hours. About 1 hour before serving, add the zucchini (courgette) and stir through half the remaining parsley. Serve sprinkled with the last of the parsley.

Grandma's Tip

Store onions in a cool, dry place away from heat and light. Hang them in a mesh bag so that air can circulate around the onions. Avoid storing onions near potatoes because the onions will absorb moisture from the potatoes.

Hearty Beef Stew

Preparation time: 30 minutes
Cooking time: 8 hours
Serves: 6

2 tablespoons oil
1kg (2lb) lean stewing beef, trimmed and cubed
2 onions, sliced
2 cloves garlic, chopped
1 eggplant (aubergine), diced
1 cup beef stock (broth)
400g (14oz) canned whole peeled tomatoes, chopped
¼ cup tapioca (sago)
1 teaspoon ground cinnamon
1 bay leaf
2 teaspoons salt
freshly ground black pepper
400g (14oz) canned chickpeas (garbanzo beans), rinsed and drained
oregano leaves, to garnish

1 Heat the oil in a large frying pan (skillet) over a medium heat. Add meat and cook
   for 5 minutes, turning occasionally. Add the onions and garlic and cook for a further
   5 minutes, stirring constantly. Drain off any excess fats. Place the beef mixture and
   eggplant (aubergine) in slow cooker.

2 Combine stock (broth) with juice from canned tomatoes, tapioca (sago), cinnamon,
   bay leaf, salt and pepper and pour into slow cooker, stirring well. Cover and cook on
   low for 8 hours.

3 Approximately 30 minutes before serving, turn to high. Stir in chickpeas (garbanzo beans)
   and tomatoes and cook for the remaining time. Serve garnished with oregano leaves.

Beef Casserole with Orange and Cider

Preparation time: 20 minutes
Cooking time: 4–8 hours
Serves: 6

3 tablespoons vegetable oil
1kg (2lb) beef blade steak, trimmed and cubed
1 large brown onion, sliced
1 clove garlic, crushed
½ cup dry cider
2 beef stock cubes (bouillon), crumbled
2 sprigs fresh thyme
2 large oranges, thickly sliced
salt and freshly ground black pepper
1 stalk celery, chopped

1 Heat oil in a frying pan (skillet) and brown meat well. Add onion and garlic and sauté until golden.

2 Place mixture in slow cooker. Add cider, stock cubes (bouillon), thyme, oranges, salt and pepper to taste, and celery. Cook on low for 6–8 hours or high for 4–5 hours and serve.

Grandma's Tip

For a milder flavour, use a white onion instead of a brown onion. White onion is a great substitute when you need an onion flavour, but don't want it to be too powerful.

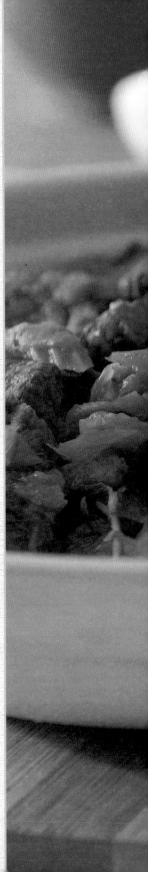

Gingered-Up Beef

Preparation time: 3 hours 25 minutes
Cooking time: 5 hours
Serves: 6

3 onions, finely chopped
1 clove garlic, crushed
4cm (1½in) piece ginger (gingerroot), finely chopped
2 teaspoons salt
½ teaspoon hot chilli (pepper) sauce
1.5kg (3lb) blade or oyster blade steak, cubed
500g (1lb) canned tomatoes, drained and chopped
1 cup beef stock (broth)

1   Place onion, garlic, ginger (gingerroot), salt and chilli (pepper) sauce in a food processor
    or blender and blend to a purée.

2   Mix meat and purée and allow to stand for at least 3 hours, turning meat occasionally.

3   Place meat in slow cooker and add tomatoes and beef stock (broth). Cook on high for
    1 hour, then on low for 4 hours or until meat is tender. Serve with rice, garnished with
    lemon quarters.

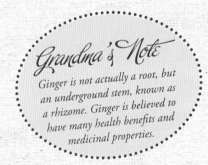

Grandma's Note

*Ginger is not actually a root, but
an underground stem, known as
a rhizome. Ginger is believed to
have many health benefits and
medicinal properties.*

Beef Pot Roast

Preparation time: 25 minutes
Cooking time: 4–7 hours
Serves: 4–6

1kg (2lb) piece beef topside
salt and freshly ground black pepper
½ cup soft wholemeal breadcrumbs
1 tomato, chopped, plus 6 peeled and sliced
2 canned anchovies, mashed
½ clove garlic, crushed
¼ cup parsley, chopped
1 teaspoon dried basil
2 small red capsicums (peppers), chopped
1 small onion, chopped, plus 2 sliced
1 tablespoon olive oil
plain (all-purpose) flour

1   Wipe meat with absorbent paper and cut a deep pocket in the side. Season inside.

2   In a bowl, mix breadcrumbs, chopped tomato, anchovies, garlic, parsley, half
    the basil, half the capsicum (pepper) and the chopped onion. Season to taste.
    Stuff mixture into pocket of beef, pressing down firmly, and sew opening together
    with coarse thread.

3   Heat oil in a frying pan (skillet) and brown meat on both sides, then place into slow
    cooker. Arrange sliced tomatoes and onions and remaining basil and capsicum on and
    around meat. Cook on high for about 4 hours or on low for 6–7 hours.

4   To serve, remove meat from liquid and keep warm, then whisk just enough flour into
    gravy to thicken it. Slice meat and serve with gravy.

Corned Silverside

Preparation time: 10 minutes
Cooking time: 8 hours
Serves: 8

2kg (4lb) piece silverside
zest of 1 orange
1 large sprig thyme
2 bay leaves
1 tablespoon Angostura bitters
12 black peppercorns

1 Place meat into slow cooker, cover with water and add orange zest, thyme, bay leaves, bitters and peppercorns.

2 Cook on low for at least 8 hours. If to be served cold, allow meat to cool in the liquid to keep it succulent.

Grandma's Tip
Fresh thyme can be stored for up to one week by wrapping it in a damp paper towel and then placing it in a sealed plastic bag in the fridge.

Beef and Red Wine Pot Roast

Preparation time: 45 minutes
Cooking time: 6–7 hours
Serves: 6–8

2kg (4lb) piece good-quality beef, trimmed of fat
2 cloves garlic, finely sliced, plus 1 clove crushed
1 tablespoon vegetable oil
1 large onion, sliced
3 tablespoons brandy
½ cup red wine
2 fresh pig's trotters, washed and roughly chopped
3 carrots, roughly chopped
2 bay leaves
3 sprigs parsley
3 sprigs thyme
salt and freshly ground black pepper

1   Wipe beef with absorbent paper. Insert the tip of a sharp knife all over the meat and
    push garlic slivers into the cuts.

2   Heat the oil in a heavy saucepan and sauté the onion until soft and golden.
    Add the meat, turning occasionally, until well browned.

3   Warm the brandy in a small saucepan, then set alight and pour it over meat. Allow to
    burn out, add the wine and leave to simmer for approximately 5 minutes. Transfer
    meat to slow cooker.

4   Add trotters, carrots, crushed garlic and herbs to slow cooker, then pour over 1 cup
    warm water or milk. Season to taste and cook on low for approximately 6 hours.
    Test for tenderness after about 5 hours – meat must not be cooked to the point where
    it falls apart. Remove meat and set aside to rest.

5   Strain stock through muslin or nylon sieve and allow to stand until fat has firmed
    on top. Carefully skim fat off, strain the liquid again. Reduce liquid until it has
    thickened slightly to make a sauce. Slice beef and serve on a platter with steamed
    vegetables and sauce.

Paprika Beef Ribs

Preparation time: 30 minutes
Cooking time: 5–8 hours
Serves: 4

2 tablespoons plain (all-purpose) flour
1 tablespoon sweet paprika
salt and freshly ground black pepper
750g (1.5lb) short beef ribs
1 tablespoon vegetable oil
3 onions, sliced
1 carrot, sliced
2 tablespoons beef stock (broth)
1 cup tomato purée (passata)
1 teaspoon sugar (optional)

1 Mix together flour, paprika, salt and pepper. Pat beef ribs dry with absorbent paper
   and rub with spice mixture.

2 Heat the oil in a frying pan (skillet) and brown the beef ribs well. Transfer to the
   slow cooker.

3 Add a little more oil to frying pan, if necessary, and sauté onion until golden brown.
   Pour contents of pan into slow cooker, add the carrot and stock (broth) and stir.

4 Combine the tomato purée (passata) and gently mix through meat and vegetables in
   slow cooker. Cook for 6–8 hours on low or 5–6 hours on high. Adjust seasoning if
   necessary, and if tomato mixture is a little sharp, add sugar. Allow dish to cool, remove
   all fat, and reheat to serve.

Chilli Beef Tacos

Preparation time: 25 minutes
Cooking time: 4–5 hours
Serves: 6

2 teaspoons vegetable oil
500g (1lb) minced (ground) beef
2 onions, chopped
60g (2oz) taco seasoning mix
½ teaspoon freshly ground black pepper
2 tablespoons tomato paste (purée)
½ cup beef stock (broth)
6 taco shells or corn tortillas

1 Heat the oil in a frying pan (skillet), and sauté the beef until browned. Add onion and
   cook until slightly softened. Stir in taco mix, pepper and tomato paste (purée) and
   cook for 1–2 minutes. Add stock (broth) and stir.

2 Transfer mixture to slow cooker and cook for approximately 4 hours on low. If mixture
   is too wet at the end of the cooking time, remove the cooker lid and cook on high until
   liquid has reduced.

3 Spoon beef mixture into heated taco shells or tortillas and serve at once with bowls of
   chopped tomatoes, cucumber, lettuce and cheese.

Grandma's Note

To make your own taco seasoning
mix, combine 2 teaspoons of onion
powder, 2 teaspoons of chilli powder,
1 teaspoon each of cumin, garlic
powder and paprika, and salt
and pepper to taste.

Spaghetti and Meatballs

Preparation time: 25 minutes
Cooking time: 4 hours
Serves: 4

500g (1lb) minced (ground) beef
2 white onions, finely chopped
1 clove garlic, crushed
1 tablespoon vegetable oil
½ teaspoon dried basil
1 bay leaf
salt and freshly ground black pepper
400g (14oz) canned tomatoes, drained
2 teaspoons Worcestershire sauce
3 tablespoons tomato paste (purée)
500g (1lb) wholemeal spaghetti
30g (1oz) parmesan cheese, grated

1 Mix together meat, onion and garlic, and roll into small balls. Heat the oil in
   a frying pan (skillet), add the meatballs and sauté until lightly browned.

2 Place meatballs into slow cooker and add all remaining ingredients, except pasta
   and cheese. Cook on low for approximately 4 hours.

3 Bring a large saucepan of salted water to the boil, add the spaghetti and cook for
   8 minutes or until just firm in the centre (al dente). Drain, then add to slow cooker
   and stir through sauce. Serve sprinkled with parmesan cheese.

Meatloaf

Preparation time: 20 minutes
Cooking time: 3–4 hours
Serves: 4

1 slice white bread
1 tablespoon milk
500g (1lb) minced (ground) beef
3 tablespoons natural yoghurt
30g (1oz) French onion soup mix
½ teaspoon mixed dried herbs
½ cup bran
3 spring (green) onions, chopped
1 egg, beaten
freshly ground black pepper

1   Soak bread in milk and squeeze dry. Mix thoroughly with all remaining ingredients.
    Spoon into a greased cake tin and cover with lid or foil.

2   Place tin in slow cooker and cook on low for approximately 4 hours or on high for
    approximately 3 hours. Serve hot or cold with a green salad.

Curried Beef

Preparation time: 20 minutes
Cooking time: 3–6 hours
Serves: 3–4

1 tablespoon vegetable oil
1kg (2lb) minced (ground) beef
2 white onions, chopped
3 carrots, finely chopped
¼ cup parsley, chopped
1 tablespoon mild curry powder
1 apple, diced
½ cup beef stock (broth)
1 stalk celery, diced

1 Heat the oil in a frying pan (skillet), add the beef and onion and sauté until browned. Drain fat from the pan, then pour all ingredients into slow cooker.

2 Cook on low for 5–6 hours (test after 4 hours) or on high for approximately 3 hours. Serve curry on a bed of cooked rice.

Grandma's Tip

To store celery, make sure it is dry, place it in a sealed plastic bag or container and keep it in the vegetable crisper in the fridge.

Beef Pie

Preparation time: 35 minutes
Cooking time: 7–9 hours
Serves: 6

2 tablespoons vegetable oil
1kg (2lb) blade or topside steak, cubed
1 onion, chopped
2 tablespoons plain (all-purpose) flour
2 beef stock cubes (bouillon), crumbled
1 teaspoon of yeast extract
1 tablespoon tomato paste (purée)
½ teaspoon salt
¼ cup parsley, chopped
1 teaspoon Worcestershire sauce
hot chilli (pepper) sauce
250g (8oz) pre-made puff pastry
2 tablespoons milk

1 Heat oil in frying pan (skillet) and brown the beef and onion, then transfer to slow
   cooker using a slotted spoon. Add the flour to the juices in the pan, brown it, and
   pour in 1 cup water. Add the stock cubes (bouillon), yeast extract, tomato paste
   (purée) and salt, and bring to the boil, stirring.

2 Pour liquid into slow cooker with the parsley, Worcestershire sauce and chilli (pepper)
   sauce to taste, and cook on low for at least 6–8 hours or overnight. Test meat for
   tenderness, then spoon beef mixture into a greased pie dish and allow to cool.

3 Preheat the oven to 190°C (375°F). Slice puff pastry into long strips. Brush rim of
   pie dish with a little milk and fit a pastry strip around the wet rim, then use remaining
   strips to create a lattice across the meat. Brush lightly with milk and bake pie for
   25–30 minutes.

Grandma's Note

Recipe makes one whole pie or
6 individual pies.

Light Vitello Tonnato

Preparation time: 40 minutes
Cooking time: 3 hours
Serves: 6

750g (1.5lb) fillet of veal, trimmed
1 cup white wine or dry cider
salt
10 peppercorns
1 bay leaf
1 clove garlic
1 teaspoon dried tarragon
1 large white onion, sliced
2 teaspoons white vinegar

Sauce
90g (3oz) canned tuna in water, drained
juice and zest of ½ lemon
½ cup coleslaw dressing
1 egg yolk
1 teaspoon seasoned pepper blend

1 Pour 1¼ cups water into slow cooker and add veal, wine or cider, salt, peppercorns, bay leaf, garlic, tarragon, onion and vinegar. Cook on low for approximately 4 hours or on high for approximately 2½–3 hours. Check for tenderness, as times will vary depending on quality of meat – do not overcook. Allow meat to cool fully, then remove from stock and slice thinly. Reserve around 2 tablespoons of the stock.

2 To make the sauce, add the tuna, lemon juice and a tablespoon of coleslaw dressing to a food processor or blender and purée.

3 Beat the egg yolk into remaining coleslaw dressing and mix in the tuna purée, pepper blend and grated lemon zest. Add reserved veal stock and blend well – the mixture should have the consistency of thin cream.

4 To serve, arrange veal in overlapping slices on a platter, then spoon over the sauce. Serve with salad.

Lamb

If you throw a lamb chop in the oven, what's to keep it from
getting done?

Joan Crawford (1905–1977), in The Women

Boiled Mutton
with Caper Sauce

Preparation time: 45 minutes
Cooking time: 6–8 hours
Serves: 6–8

1 small leg mutton
1 sprig thyme
1 bay leaf
1 sprig parsley
salt
6 peppercorns
2 large onions, sliced

Caper sauce
30g (1oz) butter
1 tablespoon plain (all-purpose) flour
½ teaspoon mustard powder
1¼ cups milk
1 spring (green) onion, chopped
2 teaspoons salted capers, rinsed
salt and freshly ground black pepper

1 Wipe mutton with absorbent paper and place in slow cooker. Add herbs, seasoning
   and sliced onions, cover with cold water and cook on low for approximately 8 hours
   or on high for approximately 6 hours, until meat is tender. Remove meat and keep
   warm. Strain off and reserve ½ cup of the cooking liquid.

2 To make the sauce, melt the butter in a small saucepan, add the flour and mustard and
   cook for a couple of minutes, stirring constantly.

3 Mix together milk and reserved cooking liquid and gradually stir into butter and flour
   mixture. Whisk until smooth, then bring to the boil, reduce heat and stir for a minute
   or two. Add spring (green) onion and capers and adjust seasoning. Slice the mutton
   and serve with caper sauce.

Lamb Shanks
with Orange

Preparation time: 30 minutes
Cooking time: 8–10 hours
Serves: 4

4 lamb shanks, trimmed of fat
2 white onions, sliced
3 oranges, sliced
1 lemon, sliced
1 cup dry white wine
½ cup chicken stock (broth)
salt and freshly ground black pepper
2 bay leaves or 1 sprig rosemary
1 tablespoon Grand Marnier

1 Place shanks in slow cooker and arrange onions, oranges and lemon between and
   around shanks.

2 Mix wine and stock (broth) and season to taste. Place bay leaves or rosemary sprig
   on shanks and pour over wine mixture. Cook on low for approximately 8 hours
   or overnight.

3 To serve, remove cooked citrus slices and bay leaves and skim off as much surface fat
   as possible. Remove shanks carefully and place on a heated serving platter, then add
   liqueur to liquid, heat through on high and pour over shanks. Garnish with extra
   half-slices of orange and fresh herbs.

Lamb Casserole

Preparation time: 35 minutes
Cooking time: 2 hours
Serves: 4

1 tablespoon olive oil
1 small eggplant (aubergine), sliced
250g (8oz) minced (ground) lamb
3 large ripe tomatoes, peeled and sliced
salt and freshly ground black pepper
6 fresh basil leaves, finely shredded
120g (4oz) Swiss cheese, grated

1 Heat the oil in a large frying pan (skillet) over medium heat. Add eggplant (aubergine) and cook until golden brown. Drain on absorbent paper.

2 Add the lamb and cook for 3–4 minutes or until browned. Drain off any excess fat.

3 In a small casserole dish that fits into your slow cooker, arrange a layer of eggplant slices, a layer of lamb and a layer of sliced tomato, and sprinkle with salt and pepper and half of the basil. Cover with grated cheese. Repeat layers until casserole dish is filled, ending with a cheese layer.

4 Place casserole in slow cooker and cook on high for approximately 2 hours.

Grandma's Note
If preferred, casserole may be placed under griller (broiler) for a minute or two to brown the cheese topping before serving.

Lancashire Hotpot

Preparation time: 20 minutes
Cooking time: 8–10 hours
Serves: 4–6

8 neck or chump lamb chops, trimmed of fat
6 carrots, peeled and thinly sliced
6 parsnips, peeled and thinly sliced
6 onions, peeled and thinly sliced
6 potatoes, peeled, parboiled and sliced
salt and freshly ground black pepper
¼ cup parsley, chopped

1 Layer all ingredients except parsley in the slow cooker, ending with a layer of potatoes. Cover with water and cook on low for 8 hours or overnight, until lamb is falling off bones. Skim off any fat.

2 To serve, ladle out the meat and vegetables, spoon over the flavoursome juices and sprinkle with parsley.

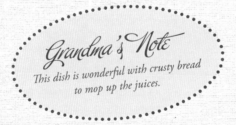

Grandma's Note
This dish is wonderful with crusty bread
to mop up the juices.

Greek Lamb with Rosemary

Preparation time: 25 minutes
Cooking time: 5–8 hours
Serves: 6

1.5kg (3lb) lamb, trimmed and cubed
1 large white onion, finely sliced
2 teaspoons dried rosemary
¼ teaspoon freshly ground black pepper
¼ teaspoon salt
1 cup chicken or veal stock (broth)
¼ cup dry white wine
1 tablespoon plain (all-purpose) flour
3 rosemary sprigs

1   Place lamb in slow cooker with all other ingredients except rosemary sprigs.
    Cook on low for approximately 6–8 hours or on high for approximately 5–6 hours.

2   If a thicker gravy is preferred, mix together some of the cooking liquid with plain
    (all-purpose) flour. Either pour mixture back into slow cooker and cook on high until
    thickened, stirring occasionally, or gently heat flour mixture on the stovetop in a small
    saucepan, whisking until thickened, before pouring back into the slow cooker.

3   Garnish with rosemary sprigs and serve.

Grandma's Note
This dish goes nicely with a glass of
chilled, pine-flavoured retsina.

Lamb and Spinach Curry

Preparation time: 40 minutes
Cooking time: 7–8 hours
Serves: 4

2 tablespoons vegetable oil
2 onions, chopped
2 cloves garlic, chopped
25mm (1in) piece fresh ginger (gingerroot), finely chopped
1 cinnamon stick
¼ teaspoon ground cloves
3 cardamom pods
750g (1.5lb) lamb, diced
1 tablespoon ground cumin
1 tablespoon ground coriander
⅓ cup natural yoghurt
2 tablespoons tomato paste (purée)
¾ cup beef stock (broth)
salt and freshly ground black pepper
120g (4oz) baby spinach, chopped
2 tablespoons blanched almonds, toasted

1 Heat the oil in a large heavy-based saucepan. Add onions, garlic, ginger (gingerroot), cinnamon, cloves and cardamom and cook for 5 minutes. Add the lamb and cook for 5 minutes, turning, until it begins to brown.

2 Transfer mixture to slow cooker set on high. Mix in the cumin and coriander, then add the yoghurt 1 tablespoon at a time, stirring well each time. Mix the tomato paste (purée) and stock (broth) together and add to the cooker. Season to taste, then reduce the heat to low and cook for 7 hours.

3 Stir in the spinach, cover and simmer for another 15 minutes or until the mixture has reduced slightly. Remove the cinnamon stick and the cardamom pods and mix in the almonds. Serve with rice.

Lamb Shanks
with Red Wine

Preparation time: 20 minutes
Cooking time: 4–10 hours
Serves: 6

6 lamb shanks
2 medium onions, chopped
2 cloves garlic, crushed
¼ cup plain (all-purpose) flour
¼ cup fresh coriander (cilantro), chopped
¼ cup beef stock (broth)
¾ cup red wine
2 tablespoons tomato paste (purée)
juice and zest of 1 orange
3 large sprigs fresh rosemary, leaves removed and chopped

1 Trim excess fat from the lamb shanks.

2 Place the onions and garlic in a slow cooker bowl. Put flour in a plastic bag with the lamb shanks, shake to completely coat the shanks and then place shanks in the cooker on top of the onions and garlic. Sprinkle any leftover flour over the top.

3 Combine all other ingredients in a small bowl and mix thoroughly, then spoon this over the shanks in the cooker.

4 Place lid on and cook on high for 4–5 hours or on low for 9–10 hours. Serve with green beans and mashed potatoes.

Slow-Cooked Lamb Roast

Preparation time: 25 minutes
Cooking time: 3–8 hours
Serves: 4

1.5kg (3lb) lamb roast
2 cloves garlic, cut into slivers
2 sprigs fresh rosemary
2 tablespoons olive oil
30g (1oz) butter
1 large onion, sliced
400g (14oz) canned butter beans, drained and rinsed
¼ cup flat-leaf parsley, chopped
½ cup chicken stock (broth)
salt and freshly ground black pepper

1 Make small incisions all over lamb with a very sharp knife, then stuff each with a sliver of garlic and a sprig of rosemary.

2 Heat oil in a large frying pan (skillet), cook lamb until browned all over. Remove from pan and transfer to slow cooker.

3 In the same pan, add butter and cook onion for 1–2 minutes or until transparent, then place in slow cooker with remaining ingredients except seasoning.

4 Cover and cook on high for 3–4 hours, or on low for 6–8 hours. Season with salt and pepper.

5 Remove meat from slow cooker and rest for 10 minutes before carving. Serve slices of lamb with beans and parsley sauce.

Easy Lamb Stew

Preparation time: 30 minutes
Cooking time: 8–11 hours
Serves: 8

1.5kg (3lb) lamb shoulder, boned and cut into 25mm (1in) cubes
500g (1lb) potatoes, cut into large cubes
4 large carrots, cut in 25mm (1in) pieces
1 medium onion, halved and thinly sliced
1 stalk celery, sliced diagonally
1 teaspoon salt
2 tablespoons freshly ground black pepper
1 bouquet garni
1 cup tomato purée (passata)
500g (1lb) frozen sliced green beans
250g (8oz) fresh mushrooms, cleaned and sliced
1 cup sour cream
1 tablespoon plain (all-purpose) flour

1   Put lamb into a large slow cooker. Add potatoes, carrots, onion, celery, salt, pepper, bouquet garni, tomato purée (passata) and 2 cups water, and mix. Cover and cook on low 8–10 hours.

2   Remove bouquet garni. Add green beans and mushrooms, then blend sour cream and flour, add to cooker and stir.

3   Cover and cook on high for 30–60 minutes.

Grandma's Note

A bouquet garni is a bundle of fresh herbs tied together. The herbs usually include parsley, thyme and bay leaves. The herbs can be tied with string or wrapped in cheesecloth to stop them from breaking up during cooking.

Poultry

If God grants me longer life, I will see to it that no peasant in my kingdom will lack the means to have a chicken in the pot every Sunday.

Henri IV of France (1553–1610)

Drunken Chicken Stew

Preparation time: 25 minutes
Cooking time: 8–10 hours
Serves: 4

1 chicken, jointed
3 rashers bacon, rinds removed
3 white onions, thickly sliced
3 carrots, thickly sliced
¼ cup parsley, chopped
1 sprig thyme
12 peppercorns
½ clove garlic, crushed
1¼ cups white wine

1   Soak chicken in salted water for 1 hour. Drain well.

2   Cut bacon into large pieces and combine with all other ingredients in slow cooker. Cook on low for 8 hours or overnight. Remove thyme sprig and serve on a bed of cooked rice, garnished with extra parsley.

Grandma's Tip

Rabbit is also delicious prepared in this way. Rabbit meat is very high in protein and low in fat.

Citrus Chicken

Preparation time: 40 minutes
Cooking time: 4–6 hours
Serves: 4–5

1 lemon
1.5kg (3lb) roasting chicken, whole
1 bouquet garni
3 carrots, thinly sliced
6 onions, thinly sliced
½ cup chicken stock (broth)
salt and freshly ground black pepper
pinch of nutmeg

Cream sauce
170g (6oz) button mushrooms, sliced
½ cup unthickened (half and half) cream

1   Halve the lemon, squeeze out the juice and brush it all over the chicken.
    Place lemon skins in the chicken cavity.

2   Lightly grease the slow cooker and add the bouquet garni. Place the chicken on top
    and arrange the carrot and onion around the outside. Pour in the stock (broth), season
    to taste, add nutmeg, then cook for approximately 6 hours on low or 4–5 hours on
    high (cooking time will vary depending on the tenderness of the chicken).

3   To make the sauce, sauté the mushrooms. Remove about ½ cup of chicken stock from
    the slow cooker, skim off as much fat as possible, and bring to the boil in a small
    saucepan. Add the stock to the mushrooms and reduce, then add the cream and
    reduce to make a pouring sauce. Serve chicken with the cream sauce.

Grandma's Note

*A bouquet garni is a bundle of fresh herbs
tied together. The herbs usually include
parsley, thyme and bay leaves. The herbs
can be tied with string or wrapped
in cheesecloth to stop them from
breaking up during cooking.*

Mustard Chicken

Preparation time: 40 minutes
Cooking time: 5–6 hours
Serves: 3–4

3 carrots, peeled and diced
3 large onions, finely chopped
1 clove garlic, crushed
2 teaspoons dried thyme
1 bay leaf
salt and seasoned pepper blend
500g (1lb) lean pork, skinned and sliced
1.5kg (3lb) chicken, jointed
4 rashers bacon, rinds removed
½ cup dry white wine
¼ cup brandy

Mustard sauce
1 egg yolk
3 tablespoons thickened (whipping) cream
1 tablespoon Dijon mustard

1   In a bowl, combine the carrot, onion, garlic, herbs and salt and pepper. Place half the pork in the base of the slow cooker, then add half the vegetable mixture. Add the chicken pieces, the remaining vegetable mixture, then the remaining pork. Place bacon rashers on top.

2   Pour over combined wine and brandy. Place a piece of foil over the slow cooker, then cover with lid and cook on low for around 5 hours (cooking time may vary depending on the tenderness of the chicken).

3   To make the sauce, drain off the cooking liquid, skim off any fat and pour into a small saucepan. Beat egg yolk and cream together, add to saucepan and whisk. Cook gently until thick, but do not allow to boil. Add the mustard and whisk until thoroughly blended.

4   Arrange chicken pieces, pork and vegetables on warmed serving platter, and pour over the mustard sauce. Serve with potatoes, sprinkled with parsley.

Grandma's Tip
Rabbit can be used in this recipe
instead of chicken.

Fricasséed Chicken with Vinegar

Preparation time: 30 minutes
Cooking time: 1½–2 hours
Serves: 4

¼ cup olive oil
1kg (2lb) chicken thigh fillets, quartered
freshly ground black pepper
2 large cloves garlic, chopped
2 sprigs fresh rosemary, leaves removed and chopped
5 anchovy fillets, chopped
½ cup white wine vinegar
2 tablespoons balsamic vinegar
20 Kalamata olives

1   In a heavy-based frying pan (skillet), heat the olive oil and brown the chicken pieces
    all over, seasoning well with pepper. Transfer to a plate and keep warm. Turn
    the heat to low and add garlic, rosemary and anchovies. Stir until the mixture
    is aromatic.

2   Transfer the garlic mixture and chicken to the slow cooker. Add the white wine
    vinegar and cook on high for about 1½ hours or until the chicken is tender. Just
    before serving, stir in the balsamic vinegar and olives.

Grandma's Tip
This dish is delicious served with
spinach and potatoes roasted in olive oil
and rosemary.

Nice'n'easy Chinese Chicken

Preparation time: 30 minutes
Cooking time: 2½–4 hours
Serves: 4

1 tablespoon vegetable oil
4 chicken pieces
2 chicken stock cubes (bouillon), crumbled
1 tablespoon cornflour (cornstarch)
2–3 tablespoons soy sauce
freshly ground black pepper
750g (1.5lb) chopped Chinese vegetables (such as bok choy, choy sum and gai lan)
3 spring (green) onions, sliced diagonally
fresh coriander (cilantro), chopped, to garnish

1   Heat the oil in a frying pan (skillet). Remove the skin from the chicken pieces, add to the pan and brown lightly.

2   Transfer chicken to slow cooker and add the stock cubes (bouillon) and ½ cup water. Cook on low for 3–4 hours or on high for approximately 2½–3½ hours (cooking time will vary depending on the tenderness of the chicken).

3   Blend the cornflour (cornstarch) with 1 tablespoon water and pour back into slow cooker, stirring thoroughly. Add soy sauce and pepper.

4   Turn the slow cooker to high, add the Chinese vegetables and cook for approximately 30 minutes. Add spring (green) onions about 15 minutes before the end. Serve with cooked rice or noodles, and sprinkle with chopped coriander (cilantro).

Easy Chicken Curry

Preparation time: 25 minutes
Cooking time: 4–6 hours
Serves: 4–5

1.5kg (3lb) chicken, jointed
60g (2oz) leek and potato soup mix
1 tablespoon curry powder
zest of ½ lemon, grated
250g (8oz) green beans, blanched
salt and freshly ground black pepper

1   Trim chicken pieces and place in slow cooker. Combine soup mix and curry powder
    and sprinkle over and around chicken pieces. Pour over enough water to barely cover
    chicken and cook on high for approximately 4 hours or on low for approximately
    6 hours.

2   About 1 hour before serving, stir in lemon zest and beans. Add salt and pepper to
    taste. Serve with cooked rice.

Grandma's Tip

For a sweeter, milder curry use garam
masala in place of the curry powder;
for a spicier curry, use a hot Madras
curry powder.

Green Chicken Curry with Lemongrass Rice

Preparation time: 35 minutes
Cooking time: 3–4 hours
Serves: 6

2 cups coconut milk
1 cup chicken stock (broth)
2 tablespoons green curry paste
3 kaffir lime leaves, shredded
200g (7oz) pumpkin, chopped
4 chicken breast fillets, cubed
120g (4oz) canned bamboo shoots, drained
120g (4oz) snake beans or green beans, chopped
200g (7oz) bok choy, chopped
1 tablespoon fish sauce
1 tablespoon grated palm sugar
¼ cup fresh Thai basil leaves, torn

Lemongrass rice
1½ cups jasmine rice
2 stalks lemongrass, bruised

1   Combine coconut milk, stock (broth), curry paste and lime leaves in a slow cooker on high. Cook until the sauce begins to thicken. Add the pumpkin and cook for 20 minutes or until it starts to soften.

2   Add the chicken and bamboo shoots and cook for 1 hour. Add the beans, bok choy, fish sauce and palm sugar and cook until the vegetables are tender, approximately 1 more hour. Stir through the basil leaves.

3   To make the lemongrass rice, put the rice, lemongrass and 4 cups water in a saucepan. Bring to the boil and cook over a high heat until steam holes appear in the top of the rice. Reduce the heat to low, cover and cook for 10 minutes or until all the liquid is absorbed and the rice is tender. Remove the lemongrass. Serve curry spooned over bowls of rice.

Ginger Chicken and Pineapple Salad

Preparation time: 35 minutes
Cooking time: 3–5 hours
Serves: 6

1.5kg (3lb) roasting chicken, whole
salt and peppercorns
2 cloves garlic
2 small white onions, sliced into rings
30g (1oz) ginger (gingerroot), grated
1 pineapple, cubed
1 red capsicum (pepper), chopped
2 tablespoons vinaigrette or coleslaw dressing
¼ cup parsley, chopped

1 Place the chicken in the slow cooker and cover with cold water. Add the salt, peppercorns, garlic and half the onion and ginger (gingerroot) and cook on low for approximately 5 hours or on high for 3 hours (cooking time will vary depending on the tenderness of the chicken – the flesh should not be falling off the bones). Remove chicken from stock and allow to cool. Retain stock for soups.

2 Shred chicken into bite-size pieces. Combine with remaining onion and ginger, pineapple and capsicum (pepper). Toss salad with dressing and garnish with parsley.

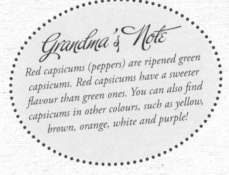

Grandma's Note

Red capsicums (peppers) are ripened green capsicums. Red capsicums have a sweeter flavour than green ones. You can also find capsicums in other colours, such as yellow, brown, orange, white and purple!

Moroccan-Style Chicken Wings

Preparation time: 40 minutes
Cooking time: 9 hours
Serves: 6

2 tablespoons vegetable oil
1kg (2lb) chicken wings
1 large onion, finely chopped
1 clove garlic, crushed
2cm (¾in) piece ginger (gingerroot), grated
½ teaspoon ground turmeric
½ teaspoon ground cumin
1 cinnamon stick
¼ cup cider vinegar
2 cups apricot nectar
salt and freshly ground black pepper
90g (3oz) pitted prunes, pitted
90g (3oz) dried apricots
1 tablespoon honey
¼ cup lemon juice
steamed couscous, to serve

1 Heat the oil in a large saucepan and brown the chicken wings in batches. Remove browned wings to a plate. Add the onion to the pan and cook for 2 minutes. Stir in the garlic and cook for a further minute.

2 Transfer the onion and garlic to the slow cooker. Add the chicken, ginger (gingerroot) and spices, and stir to coat wings with spices. Add the vinegar and apricot nectar, season to taste and cook on low for 6 hours.

3 Add the prunes, apricots, honey and lemon juice to the cooker and simmer for 2 more hours. Remove lid, turn to high and simmer for 35 minutes. If a thicker sauce is desired, remove the wings and fruit to a serving platter and simmer until the sauce reduces and thickens. Serve wings immediately on a bed of steamed couscous and pour over the sauce. Garnish with parsley.

Curried Chicken Wings

Preparation time: 35 minutes
Cooking time: 4–5 hours
Serves: 4

250g (8oz) potatoes, peeled
750g (1.5lb) chicken wings
1 tablespoon plain (all-purpose) flour
1 tablespoon curry powder
1 tablespoon vegetable oil
1 white onion, chopped
1 cup chicken stock (broth)
salt and freshly ground black pepper
250g (8oz) carrots, peeled and sliced diagonally
6 spring (green) onions, chopped (optional)

1 Parboil potatoes, cube roughly and set aside.

2 Wipe the chicken wings with absorbent paper and roll in the combined flour and curry powder. Heat the oil in a frying pan (skillet), brown the chicken, then place it in slow cooker set on low.

3 Add onion to frying pan and cook until softened, then add to slow cooker. Add the stock (broth) to the frying pan, stirring constantly until it boils and thickens. Season to taste and pour into slow cooker.

4 Add potatoes and carrots to cooker and cook for approximately 4 hours, testing after that time. Do not allow to overcook, as meat will fall from bones. Stir in spring (green) onions, if using, just before serving. Serve curry with pappadums.

Grandma's Tip

If carrots are rather old and woody, it is a good idea to lightly cook them before adding to slow cooker.

Chicken Crêpes

Preparation time: 50 minutes
Cooking time: 3–5 hours
Serves: 6–8 (about 16 crêpes)

1.5kg (3lb) roasting chicken, whole
2 chicken stock cubes (bouillon), crumbled
1 onion, chopped
3 sprigs parsley
1 sprig thyme
120g (4oz) butter
1 spring (green) onion, finely chopped
600g (21oz) button mushrooms, sliced
4 tablespoons plain (all-purpose) flour
salt and freshly ground black pepper
1½ cups milk
1 tablespoon dry sherry
2 tablespoons thickened (whipping) cream
3 hard-boiled eggs, chopped

Crêpe batter
2 cups plain (all-purpose) flour
pinch of salt
2 eggs, beaten
1 tablespoon olive oil
2 cups milk

1   Place chicken in slow cooker, add stock cubes (bouillon), onion and herbs and cover
    with water. Cook on low for 4–5 hours or high for 3–4 hours. Remove chicken and
    chop flesh finely, discarding skin and bones. Reserve ½ cup stock. Melt butter in
    frying pan (skillet) and sauté spring (green) onions and mushrooms until softened
    but not brown. Blend in flour, season and cook for 1 minute.

2   Combine the milk and reserved stock and add to the pan gradually, stirring. Add sherry
    and cream, then cook gently until stock thickens. Adjust seasoning if necessary and fold
    through cooked chicken and hard-boiled eggs. Keep mixture warm.

3   To make batter, sift the flour and salt together and make a well in the centre. Add the
    eggs, oil, and one cup of milk. Beat gradually drawing in flour from the sides. Slowly
    add remaining milk and 4 tablespoons water, making a thin batter. Cover and set aside
    for at least an hour. Heat a little butter in a heavy-based 15cm (6in) frying pan. Add
    a little batter and tilt pan so that batter spreads evenly. When cooked on one side,
    turn and cook other side. Pile crêpes in a tea towel and keep warm.

4   Preheat the oven to 180°C (350°F). Place a spoonful of chicken sauce onto each crêpe,
    roll up and place into a greased ovenproof dish. Spoon over some of the sauce and bake
    for about 10 minutes.

Duck Braised in Brandy and Port

Preparation time: 35 minutes
Cooking time: 5–6 hours
Serves: 4

1kg (2lb) plump duck
4 tablespoons plain (all-purpose) flour
60g (2oz) butter
2 tablespoons olive oil
2 rashers bacon, chopped
1 large onion, chopped
60g (2oz) small mushrooms, sliced
4 tablespoons brandy
4 tablespoons port
salt and freshly ground black pepper
½ teaspoon dried thyme

1 Pat duck dry with absorbent paper and rub lightly with 2 tablespoons flour.

2 Heat butter and oil in a frying pan (skillet) and brown duck on all sides. Remove and place in slow cooker.

3 Add a little extra butter to frying pan if necessary, then add bacon, onion and mushrooms. Sauté until golden brown. Pour half the brandy and half the port into the pan and simmer for 1–2 minutes. Add remaining flour and cook until very well browned.

4 Gradually add 1 cup water, stirring constantly. Season to taste, add thyme and spoon sauce over duck in slow cooker. Cook for approximately 5 hours on low. About 30 minutes before serving, stir remaining port and brandy into sauce around duck. Serve with green vegetables.

Fish & Seafood

Fish, to taste right, must swim three times – in water,
in butter and in wine.

Polish Proverb

Citrus and Tarragon Fish

Preparation time: 25 minutes
Cooking time: 1–2½ hours
Serves: 4

2 teaspoons butter
600g (21oz) white fish fillets
salt and freshly ground black pepper
8 large sprigs tarragon
2 oranges, each cut into four slices
2 lemons, each cut into four slices
4 tablespoons dry white wine

1 Cut four pieces of aluminium foil and lightly butter each. Place a piece of fish on each foil sheet and season to taste.

2 Lay a tarragon sprig on each piece of fish then a slice of orange and a slice of lemon side by side. Turn up the sides of the foil and spoon 1 tablespoon wine over each fish piece, then fold over the foil and seal the parcels. Place in the slow cooker and cook on high for 1–1½ hours or on low for 2–2½ hours.

3 To serve, place parcels on serving plates, open the top of each parcel and replace the cooked herb sprigs and citrus slices with fresh herb sprigs and citrus slices. Alternatively, carefully transfer the fish to the plate, replace the herbs and citrus slices, and spoon the juices over the top.

Fillets Veronique

Preparation time: 30 minutes
Cooking time: 1½–2 hours
Serves: 4

8 fillets of delicately flavoured fish
1 cup white wine
salt and freshly ground black pepper
1 bouquet garni
30g (1oz) butter
1 tablespoon cornflour (cornstarch)
½ cup thickened (whipping) cream
250g (8oz) small seedless grapes

1 Place fillets in slow cooker, cover with wine and add salt, pepper and bouquet garni.
   Cook on low for 1–1½ hours, or until fish is tender but still firm. Drain off and
   reserve liquid, and discard bouquet garni.

2 Heat the butter in a frying pan (skillet), stir in the cornflour (cornstarch) and cook
   for a couple of minutes. Combine cream and the reserved liquid and stir well. Pour
   gradually into butter and flour mixture and whisk constantly until mixture boils.
   Cook for a minute or two, stirring all the time, until sauce thickens.

3 Pour mixture back into slow cooker and turn to high. Cook for approximately
   30 minutes, add grapes and allow to heat through. Serve very hot, with sauce spooned
   over fillets and grapes piled on top.

Grandma's Note

A bouquet garni is a bundle of fresh herbs tied together. The herbs usually include parsley, thyme and bay leaves. The herbs can be tied with string or wrapped in cheesecloth to stop them from breaking up during cooking.

Smoked Cod with Lemon Herb Butter

Preparation time: 30 minutes
Cooking time: 1½–2½ hours
Serves: 6

1kg (2lb) smoked cod
a few peppercorns
½ lemon, sliced
large sprig thyme or marjoram
1 cup white wine

Lemon herb butter
120g (4oz) butter
⅓ teaspoon dried thyme
juice of ½ lemon
zest of 1 lemon, grated
¼ cup parsley, finely chopped
¼ teaspoon seasoned pepper blend

1 Cut cod into large serving pieces, removing any coarse pieces of outer skin. Place in slow cooker with remaining ingredients and add sufficient water to cover the fish.

2 Cook on low for approximately 2–2½ hours or on high for 1½–2 hours (check during cooking time to ensure that fish is not falling apart). Remove fish with a slotted spoon, arrange on a serving platter and keep warm.

3 To make the herb butter, melt butter and add all other ingredients. Spoon butter over fish to serve.

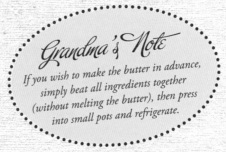

Grandma's Note

If you wish to make the butter in advance, simply beat all ingredients together (without melting the butter), then press into small pots and refrigerate.

Smoked Cod Casserole

Preparation time: 25 minutes
Cooking time: 2 hours
Serves: 6–8

1kg (2lb) cod
1 white onion, sliced
1 cup dry white wine
1 teaspoon peppercorns
1 teaspoon crushed garlic
¼ cup fennel, dill (dill weed) or aniseed, chopped
5 large tomatoes, plus 1 extra, quartered
10 black olives, pitted
6 spring (green) onions, chopped into 5cm (2in) lengths

1   Cut fish into serving-size pieces and place with onion, wine, peppercorns, garlic and
    fennel, dill (dill weed) or aniseed in the slow cooker. Cook on low for approximately
    2 hours. Check fish at the end of 1½ hours, as cooking time may vary depending on
    the tenderness of the fish and whether it has been frozen.

2   During the last 30 minutes of cooking, add four of the tomatoes and the olives.
    To serve, pour fish and juices into a casserole dish. Fold through the spring (green)
    onions and garnish with remaining tomato quarters.

Grandma's Note

*Store garlic in a cool place away from
sunlight. You also need to allow air to
circulate around garlic. Keep it in a
wire mesh basket, a paper bag or a garlic
keeper. Unbroken garlic bulbs will keep
for up to 8 weeks, but once broken they
should be used within a few days.*

Curried Scallops

Preparation time: 25 minutes
Cooking time: 2 hours
Serves: 6

250g (8oz) scallops
½ cup dry white wine
1 bouquet garni
120g (4oz) butter
1¼ cups unthickened (half and half) cream
½ teaspoon curry powder
salt and freshly ground black pepper
2 egg yolks
2 tablespoons milk

1 Place scallops, white wine and bouquet garni in the slow cooker and cook on low for approximately 1 hour. Pour off and reserve liquid, discard bouquet garni and keep scallops warm in slow cooker.

2 Put cooking liquid with butter into a small saucepan and boil hard to reduce. Stir in the cream, curry powder and salt and pepper, and again boil hard for 2–3 minutes. Remove from heat and allow to cool.

3 Beat egg yolks with milk, and carefully stir into cooled cream mixture. Pour mixture back into slow cooker with the scallops and cook on high for 45–60 minutes. To serve, place a little cooked rice in a small bowl and spoon over 3–4 scallops with a generous quantity of sauce. Serve immediately.

Grandma's Note

A bouquet garni is a bundle of fresh herbs tied together. The herbs usually include parsley, thyme and bay leaves. The herbs can be tied with string or wrapped in cheesecloth to stop them from breaking up during cooking.

Slow Paella

Preparation time: 35 minutes
Cooking time: 60–80 minutes
Serves: 8

1 tablespoon olive oil
2 onions, chopped
2 cloves garlic, crushed
4 sprigs fresh thyme, leaves removed and stalks discarded
zest of 1 lemon, finely grated
4 ripe tomatoes, chopped
2½ cups short-grain white rice
pinch of saffron threads, soaked in 2 cups water
5 cups chicken or fish stock (broth), warmed
290g (10oz) peas
2 red capsicums (peppers), chopped
1kg (2lb) mussels, scrubbed and debearded
500g (1lb) firm white fish fillets, chopped
290g (10oz) raw prawns (shrimps), shelled
250g (8oz) scallops
3 calamari, cleaned and sliced
¼ cup parsley, chopped

1   Preheat slow cooker on high. Add the oil and the onion and stir, then add the garlic, thyme, lemon zest and tomatoes and cook for 15 minutes.

2   Add the rice and saffron mixture and warmed stock (broth). Simmer, stirring occasionally, for 1½ hours or until the rice has absorbed almost all the liquid.

3   Stir in the peas, capsicums (peppers) and mussels and cook for 20 minutes. Add the fish, prawns (shrimps) and scallops and cook for 20 minutes. Stir in the calamari and parsley and cook for 20 minutes longer or until the seafood is cooked.

Vegetarian

Vegetables when not sufficiently cooked are known to be so
exceedingly unwholesome and indigestible, that the custom of
serving them 'crisp' should be altogether disregarded when health
is considered of more importance than fashion.

From Modern Cookery for Private Families, written by
Eliza Acton (1799–1859)

Spinach Custards

Preparation time: 35 minutes
Cooking time: 1½–2½ hours
Serves: 6–8

250g (8oz) cooked spinach or silverbeet, stems removed
120g (4oz) cream cheese
2 small eggs
½ cup milk
1 small onion, peeled and chopped
¼ teaspoon salt
freshly ground black pepper
½ teaspoon dried basil
30g (1oz) parmesan cheese, grated, pluse extra to garnish
8 fresh basil sprigs

1 Drain spinach or silverbeet until as dry as possible, then process in a food processor or blender until finely chopped. Add remaining ingredients and half the basil and blend until very smooth.

2 Pour mixture into 6–8 small, buttered ovenproof dishes and cover each with aluminium foil. Place dishes in the slow cooker and pour a little water into base, then cook on high for approximately 1½ hours or on low for 2½ hours.

3 To serve, sprinkle with extra grated cheese and garnish with a basil sprig.

Grandma's Note
This dish makes a delicious light lunch served with a salad and fresh, warm bread.

Vegetable Casserole

Preparation time: 35 minutes
Cooking time: 3–5 hours
Serves: 8

500g (1lb) potatoes, peeled and thickly sliced
500g (1lb) very ripe tomatoes, peeled and sliced
½ teaspoon sugar
2 white onions, thinly sliced
2 green or red capsicums (peppers), thinly sliced
1kg (2lb) small zucchini (courgette), sliced
salt and freshly ground black pepper
1 clove garlic, crushed
1 teaspoon dried basil
30g (1oz) butter
30g (1oz) parmesan cheese, grated
¼ cup parsley, chopped

1   Boil the potatoes until slightly tender. Sprinkle the tomatoes with sugar.

2   Grease the base of the slow cooker and layer in the vegetables, starting with the onion.
    Sprinkle each layer with salt, pepper, garlic and basil. Finish with a layer of tomatoes,
    then dot with butter. Pour over any juice from tomato slices.

3   Cook on high for approximately 3 hours or on low for approximately 5 hours.
    Serve sprinkled with grated cheese and parsley.

Grandma's Note
Zucchini (courgette) is a good source
of minerals, and vitamins A and C.
Zucchini also contains folate and fibre.

Stuffed Vine Leaves in Tomato Sauce

Preparation time: 40 minutes
Cooking time: 1½–2½ hours
Serves: 4

12 grape vine leaves, canned or fresh
olive oil
2 cups cooked brown rice
1 teaspoon dried mixed herbs
pinch of nutmeg
salt and freshly ground black pepper
1 teaspoon dried garlic
2 tomatoes, chopped and peeled
¼ cup parsley, chopped
½ teaspoon Angostura bitters (optional)
2 spring (green) onions, chopped finely

Tomato sauce
15g (0.5oz) butter
1 onion, diced
400g (14oz) canned Roma tomatoes, drained and chopped
2 teaspoons brown sugar
pinch of dried herbs
1 tablespoon tomato paste (purée)
3 tablespoons dry red wine
¼ cup parsley, chopped

1 If you are using fresh vine leaves, remove the stems, pour boiling water over leaves and
   leave for 1–2 minutes until softened. Dry and lightly wipe each leaf with a drop of oil.

2 Combine all other ingredients to make the filling. Squeeze a handful of filling to make
   it firm and place onto leaf, then fold into neat little parcel, sealing with a little squeeze.
   Repeat with remaining leaves. Arrange carefully in base of slow cooker.

3 To make the tomato sauce, heat the butter in a frying pan (skillet) and cook the onion
   until golden brown. Add all other ingredients and cook until blended. Spoon sauce
   into slow cooker over vine leaf parcels and cook on high for approximately 1½ hours
   or on low for 2–2½ hours.

Herbed Cannelloni with Tomato Sauce

Preparation time: 25 minutes
Cooking time: 1½–2½ hours
Serves: 3–4

8 instant cannelloni tubes
250g (8oz) cottage cheese
30g (1oz) parmesan cheese, grated
1 teaspoon mixed dried herbs
6 spring (green) onions, finely chopped
salt and freshly ground black pepper
few drops Angostura bitters (optional)
parmesan cheese, shared, to serve
parsley sprigs, to serve

Tomato sauce
1 cup tomato purée (passata)
3–4 spring (green) onions, chopped
2 teaspoons Worcestershire sauce
4 drops Angostura bitters
1 large clove garlic, crushed

1 Bring a large saucepan of salted water to the boil, add the pasta tubes and cook for 8 minutes or until just firm in the centre (al dente). Drain, set aside and keep warm. Place the cheese, herbs, onions, salt, pepper and bitters in a bowl and mix thoroughly.

2 To make the sauce, mix together all ingredients.

3 Lightly butter the base of the slow cooker. Spoon cheese mixture into cannelloni tubes. Spoon a little tomato sauce into the cooker, then arrange the stuffed cannelloni tubes in the cooker and spoon over remainder of sauce. Cook for 1–1½ hours on high or 2–2½ hours on low. Serve sprinkled with extra parmesan cheese and parsley sprigs.

Mushroom Casserole

Preparation time: 35 minutes
Cooking time: 1–3 hours
Serves: 4

60g (2oz) butter
1kg (2lb) mushrooms, sliced
10 spring (green) onions, chopped into 25mm (1in) lengths
60g (2oz) French onion soup mix
freshly ground black pepper
1 tablespoon sweet paprika
1–1½ cups sour cream
½ cup parsley, finely chopped

1   Heat butter in a large frying pan (skillet), add mushrooms and spring (green) onions
    and sauté for approximately 10 minutes. Add onion soup mix, stir through and cook
    for about 5 minutes.

2   Mix together pepper, paprika and sour cream and stir into mushroom mixture. Spoon
    mixture into slow cooker and cook on high for approximately 1–1½ hours or on low
    for 2–3 hours. Just before serving, stir in chopped parsley. Serve with brown rice.

Grandma's Note

*Store mushrooms in a paper bag because
the bag will absorb moisture from the
mushrooms. Keep them on a shelf in
the fridge because the vegetable
crisper is too moist.*

Argentinean Bean and Vegetable Stew

Preparation time: 35 minutes
Cooking time: 1½–2½ hours
Serves: 4

1 tablespoon olive oil
1 onion, finely diced
2 cloves garlic, crushed
1 red capsicum (pepper), diced
1 jalapeño chilli, deseeded and diced
1 teaspoon sweet paprika
400g (14oz) canned diced tomatoes
2 cups vegetable stock (broth)
250g (8oz) chat (new) potatoes, quartered
250g (8oz) sweet potato, diced
1 carrot, sliced
400g (14oz) canned cannellini (white kidney) beans, rinsed and drained
200g (7oz) Savoy cabbage, shredded
¼ cup fresh coriander (cilantro), chopped
salt and freshly ground black pepper

1 Heat oil in a large frying pan (skillet) over medium heat. Cook onion, garlic, capsicum
   (pepper) and chilli until soft. Add sweet paprika and cook until aromatic.

2 Transfer contents of frying pan to a slow cooker set on high and add tomatoes and
   vegetable stock (broth). Stir to combine, then add potato, sweet potato and carrot.
   Bring to the boil. Reduce heat to low, cover, and simmer for 1½ hours until vegetables
   are tender.

3 Add beans, cabbage and coriander (cilantro) and season with salt and pepper. Simmer
   for a further 30 minutes or until cabbage is cooked.

Grandma's Note
This dish is delicious with crusty bread.

Summer Vegetable Casserole

Preparation time: 90 minutes
Cooking time: 4 hours
Serves: 4

1 medium eggplant (aubergine), cubed
salt
250g (8oz) tomatoes, sliced
2 cloves garlic, crushed
¼ teaspoon Cayenne pepper or dash of hot chilli (pepper) sauce
1cm (½in) ginger (gingerroot), grated
1 teaspoon ground coriander
2 bay leaves
1 tablespoon raw sugar
½ cup natural yoghurt
Wholemeal (whole wheat) breadcrumbs (optional)
1 teaspoon butter (optional)

1 Cover eggplant (aubergine) with a handful of salt and allow to stand for approximately 1 hour. Rinse and drain well.

2 Combine eggplant with all remaining ingredients except yoghurt. Spoon into slow cooker and cook on low for approximately 4 hours. Test to see whether eggplant is cooked.

3 Turn setting to high, stir in the yoghurt and heat through. Remove bay leaves and serve. Each serving may be sprinkled with wholemeal (whole wheat) breadcrumbs fried in a little butter, if desired.

Moroccan Root Vegetable Curry

Preparation time: 30 minutes
Cooking time: 3½ hours
Serves: 4

1 tablespoon olive oil
1 onion, chopped
1 green chilli, deseeded and chopped
1 clove garlic, finely chopped
25mm (1in) piece ginger (gingerroot), grated
2 tablespoons plain (all-purpose) flour
2 teaspoons ground coriander
2 teaspoons ground cumin
2 teaspoons ground turmeric
1 cup vegetable stock (broth)
1 cup tomato purée (passata)
750g (1.5lb) mixed root vegetables, such as potato, sweet potato, celeriac and
    swede (rutabaga), diced
2 carrots, thinly sliced
freshly ground black pepper
steamed couscous and coriander (cilantro), to serve

1 Heat the oil in a large saucepan. Add the onion, chilli, garlic and ginger (gingerroot)
   and cook, stirring occasionally, for 3 minutes. Stir in the flour, coriander, cumin and
   turmeric and cook gently, stirring, for 2 minutes to release the flavours.

2 Transfer mixture to a slow cooker and stir in the stock (broth), then add the tomato
   purée (passata), diced root vegetables and carrots. Season with pepper and mix well.
   Cook on high for 3¼ hours or until the vegetables are tender. Serve with steamed
   couscous and garnish with coriander (cilantro).

Leeks with Beans

Preparation time: 25 minutes
Cooking time: 4–9 hours
Serves: 6

250g (8oz) dried black eyed (navy) beans, soaked overnight
1 tablespoon vegetable oil
1 large onion, chopped
2 cloves garlic, crushed
500g (1lb) leeks, sliced and washed
¼ cup parsley, chopped, plus extra to garnish
6 tomatoes, peeled, deseeded and chopped
1 tablespoon raw sugar
1 teaspoon mustard powder
2 bay leaves
½ teaspoon dried marjoram
1 tablespoon tomato paste (purée)
¼ cup vegetable stock (broth)
salt and freshly ground black pepper

1   Drain the beans well. Heat the oil in a frying pan (skillet) and sauté the onion and
    garlic, then add the leeks and sauté until softened. Spoon leek mixture, beans and
    all remaining ingredients into slow cooker.

2   Cover and cook on low for approximately 8–9 hours or on high for 4–5 hours.
    Garnish with extra parsley.

Baking

The smell of good bread baking, like the sound of lightly flowing water, is indescribable in its evocation of innocence and delight.

M. F. K. Fisher (1908–1992)

Apple and Raisin Shorties

Preparation time: 40 minutes
Cooking time: 3–4 hours
Makes: 10–12

500g (1lb) cooking apples, peeled and thinly sliced
¼ cup raw sugar
4 cloves
½ cup dark raisins
zest of 1 lemon
squeeze of lemon juice
icing (confectioner's) sugar, to finish

Pastry
150g (5oz) butter
250g (8oz) plain (all-purpose) flour
8 teaspoons wholemeal (whole wheat) flour
½ teaspoon baking powder
½ teaspoon cinnamon

1 To make pastry, rub butter into combined flour, baking powder and cinnamon.
   Add a little water and knead very lightly to a manageable dough. Set aside to cool.

2 Place apples in slow cooker with 1 tablespoon water and all other filling ingredients
   and cook for around 3 hours on low or until apples are tender. Test apples from time
   to time. Remove cloves and if mixture is too wet, drain. Allow to cool.

3 Preheat the oven to 200°C (400°F). Roll out the pastry on a floured board and cut out
   10–12 pastry bases and the same numbers of tops. Line small, greased cupcake tins
   with pastry bases, spoon in a little filling, then press tops into place and make a vent
   hole in the crust. Bake for about 45 minutes.

4 Sprinkle shorties with a little icing (confectioner's) sugar and serve either hot with
   cream as a dessert or cold as an afternoon treat.

Yoghurt Banana Bread

Preparation time: 40 minutes
Cooking time: 3 hours
Makes: 1 loaf

60g (2oz) butter
120g (4oz) caster (berry) sugar
1 egg, lightly beaten
2 large bananas, pulped
250g (8oz) self-raising wholemeal (whole wheat) flour
pinch of salt
120g (4oz) walnuts, roughly chopped
3 tablespoons natural yoghurt
cinnamon and icing (confectioner's) sugar, to finish

1 Cream together the butter and caster (berry) sugar. Add egg and banana pulp and
   mix thoroughly.

2 Mix flour and salt together and add walnuts. Add flour mixture and yoghurt
   alternately to the banana mixture in small quantities and blend thoroughly.

3 Grease a 12 x 22cm (4½ x 8½in) loaf tin, spoon in mixture and cover with lid. Place in
   slow cooker and cook on high for approximately 2½–3 hours or until a skewer inserted
   in the banana bread comes out clean. Allow to cool for 10 minutes then turn out onto
   a wire rack to cool fully.

4 Sprinkle with mixed cinnamon and icing (confectioner's) sugar and serve sliced and
   spread with butter.

Cherry and Walnut Fruit Cake

Preparation time: 30 minutes
Cooking time: 5 hours
Makes: 1 cake

250g (8oz) butter
250g (8oz) brown sugar
5 eggs, beaten to a froth
500g (1lb) sultanas (golden raisins)
170g (6oz) glacé (glazed) cherries
120g (4oz) walnut pieces
200g (7oz) plain (all-purpose) flour
1 tablespoon milk

1   Cream the butter and sugar in a bowl. Add eggs gradually. Fold in fruit, walnuts and
    flour, then add milk.

2   Grease a 22cm (8½in) springform cake tin and line its sides and base with baking
    paper. Spoon in the cake mixture, cover and place in slow cooker. Cook on high for
    4½–5 hours, taking care not to remove either the cooker or the cake tin lid until the
    last hour of cooking.

Grandma's Note

Walnuts are high in protein, omega-3 fatty acids, monounsaturated fats and fibre. They also contain a wide variety of vitamins and minerals.

Rich Berry Dessert Cake

Preparation time: 30 minutes
Cooking time: 3 hours
Serves: 8

120g (4oz) butter
¼ cup white sugar
1½ teaspoons vanilla extract
2 eggs, lightly beaten
2 cups plain (all-purpose) flour
2 teaspoons baking powder
salt
1 teaspoon mixed spice
½ cup milk
¾ cup berries of your choice
cinnamon and icing (confectioner's) sugar, to finish
thickened (whipping) cream, to serve

1   Cream the butter, sugar and vanilla, then fold eggs into mixture.

2   Sift flour, baking powder and salt together and stir in mixed spice. Add spiced flour and milk alternately to the butter mixture, folding in gently and commencing and concluding with the flour. Spoon into a greased and floured 20cm (8in) springform cake tin, smooth the surface and arrange berries on top.

3   Cover and place in slow cooker. Cook on high for approximately 3 hours, taking care not to remove either the cooker or the cake tin lid until the last hour of cooking. Sprinkle with cinnamon and icing (confectioner's) sugar and serve hot or cold, with thickened (whipping) cream.

Viennese Coffee Cake

Preparation time: 30 minutes
Cooking time: 2½ hours
Serves: 8

130g (4½oz) butter
¾ cup caster (berry) sugar
½ teaspoon vanilla extract
3 eggs
1½ cups plain (all-purpose) flour, sifted
1½ teaspoons baking powder
pinch of salt
1 tablespoon milk

Coffee syrup
1 cup strong black coffee
⅓ cup raw sugar
2 tablespoons brandy or whisky
cream, to serve

1 Beat the butter until softened, then gradually beat in the sugar and vanilla until
   mixture is light and fluffy. Add eggs one at a time, beating well after each.

2 Sift together flour, baking powder and salt and fold into butter mixture. Add milk –
   mixture should have a dropping consistency. Spoon into a greased 20cm (8in)
   springform cake tin, cover, and place tin in slow cooker. Cook on high for about
   2–2½ hours, taking care not to remove either the cooker or the cake tin lid until the
   last 1½ hours of cooking time.

3 Remove tin from slow cooker, allow to cool for about 10 minutes, then turn cake out
   of tin and allow to cool on a wire rack. When cold, replace in tin.

4 To make the coffee syrup, place the coffee into a saucepan, add sugar and ⅔ cup water
   and heat until sugar dissolves. Add the brandy or whisky and bring to the boil, stirring
   occasionally. Boil for 3 minutes. Allow to cool.

5 Pour cold syrup over cake and refrigerate overnight. Serve with cream.

Herb Bread

Preparation time: 40 minutes
Cooking time: 2–3 hours
Makes: 1 loaf

1 tablespoon compressed yeast
1 teaspoon white sugar
500g (1lb) plain (all-purpose) flour
1 teaspoon vegetable or garlic salt
2 teaspoons dried mixed herbs
2 teaspoons dried chives, crumbled
2 sprigs parsley, chopped
30g (1oz) butter

1   Crumble the yeast into a bowl, stir in sugar and 1¼ cups lukewarm water until
    yeast has dissolved. Sprinkle with a little of the flour and stand in a warm spot until
    mixture froths.

2   Mix together flour, salt and herbs. Rub in the butter, then make a well in the centre of
    the dry ingredients and pour in frothy yeast mixture. Stir well with a wooden spoon,
    then turn out onto a floured board and knead for about 5 minutes. Shape into a
    round, place back into bowl and set aside on a slow cooker set on low until dough has
    doubled in size.

3   Punch down risen dough and form into a round. Place in a greased 22cm (8½in)
    springform cake tin and set aside on the slow cooker again until dough has doubled
    in size.

4   Cover tin, place in the slow cooker and cook on high for 2–3 hours, taking care
    not to remove either the cooker or the cake tin lid until the last hour of cooking time.
    Turn loaf out and allow to cool on a wire rack. Serve dusted with a little extra flour.

Grandma's Note

*Place the dough on your warm slow
cooker to gently coax along the
proving (rising) of the dough.*

Cracked Wheat
One-Rise Bread

Preparation time: 90 minutes
Cooking time: 2 hours
Makes: 1 loaf

45g (1½oz) compressed yeast
1 tablespoon blackstrap molasses (treacle)
500g (1lb) wholemeal (whole wheat) flour
250g (8oz) plain (all-purpose) flour
¾ cup cracked wheat
1 teaspoon salt

1 In a large bowl, blend together yeast and blackstrap molasses (treacle), then add
   2 cups warm water. Mix well, sprinkle a little flour onto surface and set aside in a
   slow cooker set on low until mixture froths.

2 Mix together all dry ingredients. Pour in frothy yeast mixture and stir with a wooden
   spoon, then turn out onto a floured board and knead for at least 5 minutes, until
   mixture is smooth and pliable. Shape into a rough loaf, place in a greased 12 x 22cm
   (4½ x 8½in) loaf tin and set aside on the slow cooker (still set on low) until dough has
   doubled in size.

3 Preheat the oven to 200°C (400°F). Bake the bread for 10 minutes, then reduce
   temperature to 190°C (375°F). Continue baking for about another 40 minutes, then
   test loaf – when cooked, loaf will give a hollow sound when rapped with knuckles.
   Turn loaf out of tin and allow to cool on a wire rack.

Half and Half Loaf

Preparation time: 90 minutes
Cooking time: 2 hours
Makes: 2 loaves

2 tablespoons compressed yeast
2 teaspoons molasses (treacle) or honey
2⅓ cups warm milk
500g (1lb) plain (all-purpose) flour
500g (1lb) wholemeal (whole wheat) flour
1 tablespoon baking powder
1 tablespoon salt
60g (2oz) butter
6 tablespoons sesame seeds
1 egg white

1 Blend together yeast and molasses (treacle) or honey, then add the milk. Sprinkle a little of the flour on top of the liquid. Stand bowl in a warm spot until mixture froths.

2 Mix together the flours, baking powder and salt. Rub in the butter. Make a well in centre of the dry ingredients and pour in the frothy yeast mixture. Stir well with a wooden spoon, then turn out onto a floured board and knead for about 5 minutes. Shape into a round, place back into bowl and set aside on a slow cooker set on low until dough has doubled in size.

3 Grease two 500g (1lb) bread tins and sprinkle half the sesame seeds around base and sides of tin. Punch down risen dough and form into two rough loaves, then place in tins. Set aside on the slow cooker again until dough has risen to the top of the tins.

4 Preheat the oven to 200°C (400°F). Brush risen loaves with egg white and sprinkle with sesame seeds, then place into oven on middle shelf. Bake for 10 minutes, then reduce temperature to 175°C (350°F) and bake for a further 40–45 minutes. Turn loaves out of tins and allow to cool on a wire rack.

Desserts

Life is uncertain. Eat dessert first.

Ernestine Ulmer (1892–1987)

Apricot Mousse

Preparation time: 90 minutes
Cooking time: 2–4 hours
Serves: 4

250g (8oz) dried apricots
2 floury cooking apples, peeled and thinly sliced
juice and zest of 1 lemon
¼ cup raw sugar
3 egg whites
½ cup thickened (whipping) cream, whipped, plus extra to serve
orange zest, grated, to garnish

1   Soak dried apricots for approximately 1 hour, then drain well. Place into slow cooker
    with apples, lemon juice, zest and sugar. Cook on low for 3–4 hours or on high for
    2–3 hours, until apricots are soft and apples cooked. Drain fruit, discarding liquid,
    and purée in a blender or food processor. Chill.

2   Beat egg whites until stiff. Beat the cream in a separate bowl, then fold half the cream
    into the egg whites. Carefully fold egg white mixture and remaining cream through
    the fruit purée. Chill. Serve mousse with extra cream and a little grated orange zest.

Grandma's Tip

*If apricots are in season, you can
use 10 peeled and pitted fresh
apricots instead of dried apricots.
The fresh apricots don't need
to be soaked first.*

Ginger Custard with Choc-Ginger Sauce

Preparation time: 35 minutes
Cooking time: 1½–2½ hours
Serves: 2–3

2 large eggs
1¼ cups milk
1 tablespoon sugar
1 tablespoon preserved ginger, finely chopped
½ teaspoon ground ginger
¼ teaspoon ground cinnamon

Choc-ginger sauce
30g (1oz) dark (semi-sweet) chocolate, grated
2 teaspoons sugar
1 tablespoon ginger wine
⅔ cup evaporated milk
2 teaspoons cornflour (cornstarch)

1 To make the sauce, combine the grated chocolate, sugar, ginger wine and half the milk
in a small saucepan. Heat gently until chocolate melts, stirring constantly.

2 Mix the cornflour (cornstarch) into the remaining milk, then add to the chocolate
mixture and whisk until sauce boils. Reduce heat and simmer for approximately
3 minutes.

3 To make the custard, beat together eggs, milk and sugar, then stir in chopped ginger.
Pour into 2–3 small ovenproof dishes. Sprinkle each dish with a little ginger and
cinnamon, then cover with aluminium foil, place in slow cooker and cook for
approximately 1½ hours on high or 2–2½ hours on low. Serve custards drizzled with
hot choc-ginger sauce.

Butterscotch and Apricot Parfait

Preparation time: 40 minutes
Cooking time: 5–6 hours
Serves: 4–6

500g (1lb) fresh apricots
1 tablespoon sugar
1 cinnamon stick
pinch of ground nutmeg
1–2 ripe mangoes, peeled and sliced
½ cup thickened (whipping) cream, whipped
4 sprigs mint

Butterscotch custard
4 egg yolks
400g (14oz) canned evaporated skim milk
1 teaspoon vanilla extract
1 heaped tablespoon dark sugar

1   To make the custard, beat together all the ingredients until sugar has dissolved, then
    pour into a greased heatproof basin. Cover basin tightly with foil, place in slow cooker,
    and pour enough water into cooker to come halfway up the sides of the basin. Cook
    on low for 3–4 hours. Remove basin from slow cooker, loosen around the rim of the
    basin with a knife and slip custard onto a warmed plate.

2   Wash and stone the apricots, then place them in the slow cooker with sugar, cinnamon
    stick, nutmeg, and 1 tablespoon water to prevent sticking. Cook on high for at least
    2 hours, until tender and almost mushy. Remove cinnamon stick and drain fruit.

3   Set aside 4–6 mango slices for garnish, then layer apricots, butterscotch custard and
    mangoes in tall parfait glasses until full. Top each glass with a swirl of cream, the
    remaining mango slices and a sprig of mint.

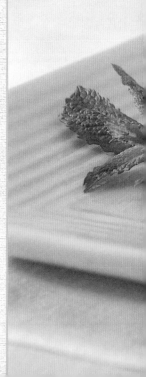

Ripe Fruit Compote

Preparation time: 10 minutes
Cooking time: 1–3 hours
Serves: 4

6 apricots, halved and stoned
150g (5oz) cherries
6 fresh plums
1 apple, sliced
½ cup sugar
rind of 1 orange
3 cloves
whipped cream, to serve

1   Combine all ingredients in the slow cooker and cook on low for 2–3 hours or on high
    for 1–1½ hours. Remove cloves and orange rind and test for sweetness, adding sugar
    or honey to taste.

2   Allow to cool, then serve with cream.

Grandma's Note

This is a marvellous recipe for
using up overripe fruit.

Cherries Grand Marnier

Preparation time: 15 minutes
Cooking time: 1 hour
Serves: 8

1¼kg (44oz) canned cherries
rind of 1 orange
2 cinnamon sticks
4 tablespoons Grand Marnier
vanilla ice cream, to serve
grated chocolate, to garnish

1 Drain cherries and retain half the syrup. Pour cherries, retained syrup, orange rind and cinnamon sticks into the slow cooker and cook on low for approximately 1 hour. Add half the Grand Marnier and heat through. Remove the cinnamon and orange rind.

2 Serve in individual bowls topped with a scoop of ice cream, a spoonful of the remaining Grand Marnier and a sprinkle of grated chocolate.

Grandma's Note

Alternatively, for a dinner party, serve the cherries in a large bowl and pour heated flaming Grand Marnier over the cherries at the table.

Dundee Marmalade Pudding

Preparation time: 25 minutes
Cooking time: 3 hours
Serves: 4–6

2 cups milk
120g (4oz) fresh, fine breadcrumbs
3 eggs, separated
60g (2oz) caster (berry) sugar
2 tablespoons dark marmalade
hot custard, to serve

1   Bring milk to the boil and pour over breadcrumbs. Allow to cool.

2   Beat the egg yolks with the sugar, then add the marmalade. Stir into the cold bread and milk mixture. Beat the egg whites until stiff and fold in.

3   Grease a pudding basin and lightly spoon in the pudding mixture. Cover basin tightly with foil and tie with kitchen string, forming a loop at the top so that the basin may be easily removed from the slow cooker. Place basin into cooker, pour over boiling water and cook on high for about 3 hours.

4   Remove basin, carefully turn out pudding and serve with hot custard.

Lemon Pudding

Preparation time: 40 minutes
Cooking time: 2–3 hours
Serves: 4

1 cup uncooked sago (tapioca)
1 large egg
1 cup milk
1–2 tablespoons raw sugar
1 teaspoon vanilla extract
½ teaspoon ground nutmeg
zest of 1 lemon, grated

1 Bring 1 cup water to a fast boil and pour in the sago (tapioca). Cook at a quick simmer, stirring often, until sago is translucent (about 15 minutes). If the water is absorbed before the sago is cooked, add a little more. When done, pour the sago into a bowl and allow to cool.

2 Beat together the egg, milk and sugar in a bowl, then add remaining ingredients and sago. Pour mixture into a lightly greased dish, sprinkle with extra nutmeg and cover with a lid or foil.

3 Place dish in the slow cooker, and carefully pour enough hot water around the dish to come three-quarters of the way up its sides. Cook on high for 2 hours or on low for 3 hours.

Grandma's Note
Serve hot or cold with stewed fruit
and whipped cream.

Creamy Rice Pudding

Preparation time: 30 minutes
Cooking time: 1–6 hours
Serves: 6

zest of 1 orange, grated
2½ cups cooked rice
1 cup evaporated milk or 1 cup ordinary milk plus 1 beaten egg
⅔ cup raw sugar
60g (2oz) butter, softened
½ teaspoon vanilla extract
½ teaspoon ground cinnamon or nutmeg
⅓ cup sultanas (golden raisins)
cream, to serve

1 Reserve a little orange zest to garnish, then mix the rice with all other ingredients. Lightly grease the slow cooker interior and spoon in pudding mixture.

2 Cook on high for approximately 1–2 hours or on low for 4–6 hours. Stir occasionally during first hour of cooking. Serve with a little cream and a pinch of grated orange zest.

Grandma's Note

Cinnamon is prepared from the inner bark of cinnamon trees. It is a fragrant, sweet spice. Nutmeg is a spice ground from the hard seeds of nutmeg tree fruit. It is also fragrant and sweet but slightly spicy.

Caramel Rice and Apricot Pudding

Preparation time: 15 minutes
Cooking time: 1½–6 hours
Serves: 6

1 cup evaporated milk
1 teaspoon vanilla extract
⅔ cup soft brown sugar
2½ cups rice, cooked but still slightly firm
60g (2oz) butter, melted
½ teaspoon mixed spice
½ cup canned apricots, drained

1 Beat together evaporated milk, vanilla and sugar. Combine with remaining ingredients, pour mixture into a greased ovenproof dish and cover with foil.

2 Place dish in slow cooker and cook on high for 1½–2 hours or on low for 4–6 hours. Stir occasionally during the first 30 minutes or so of cooking.

Grandma's Tip

This dish is best served hot. For a sweeter flavour, sprinkle with cinnamon mixed with sugar before serving.

Baked Bread and Butter Pudding

Preparation time: 45 minutes
Cooking time: 3–4 hours
Serves: 6

4 thin slices stale brown or white bread, buttered
½ cup mixed sultanas (golden raisins) and currants
3 tablespoons raw sugar
½ teaspoon grated nutmeg or cinnamon
2 eggs
2½ cups milk
1 teaspoon vanilla extract
zest of ½ orange, grated

1   Remove crusts from bread and cut into thick fingers. Grease an ovenproof dish
    and arrange bread in layers, buttered-side up. Sprinkle layers with dried fruit, sugar
    and spice.

2   Beat together eggs, milk and vanilla and stir in orange zest. Pour mixture over layered
    bread and allow to stand for approximately 30 minutes. Cover dish with lid or foil.

3   Pour 1 cup hot water into the slow cooker, then insert the pudding dish and cook on
    high for 3–4 hours.

Country Currant Pie

Preparation time: 40 minutes
Cooking time: 1–2 hours
Serves: 6–8

340g (12oz) currants
½ cup sugar
1 tablespoon cornflour (cornstarch)
juice and zest of 1 lemon
caster (berry) sugar, to finish
cream, to serve

Pastry
150g (5oz) butter
1½ cups plain (all-purpose) flour
1½ teaspoons baking powder

1   To make the pastry, place the butter in a large bowl, pour in 2 tablespoons boiling
    water and mash the butter slightly. Sift in the flour and baking powder and stir until
    mixture comes together, adding a little more flour if necessary until pastry is smooth
    and manageable. Allow to stand until firm and easy to handle.

2   Combine currants, sugar, cornflour (cornstarch), lemon juice and zest with ½ cup
    water in the slow cooker. Cook for around 1 hour on high (this filling must be cooked
    on high to ensure the cornflour cells burst and thicken it). Allow to cool.

3   Preheat the oven to 200°C (400°F). Reserve one-third of the pastry for the pie lid and
    roll out the remainder roughly on a floured board. Grease a 20cm (8in) pie dish and
    press pastry into the base and sides, then spoon in the currant filling.

4   Roll the reserved pastry out between two sheets of baking paper. Peel off one sheet of
    the paper, invert the pastry onto the pie, then remove the remaining sheet. Pinch the
    pie edges together, trim any excess, and use the pastry scraps to create a decoration for
    the lid. Sprinkle with caster (berry) sugar and bake for approximately 45–50 minutes.
    Serve with cream.

Orange-Wheel Steamed Pudding

Preparation time: 75 minutes
Cooking time: 5 hours
Serves: 6–8

2 oranges, peeled and thickly sliced, plus zest of 1 orange
90g (3oz) butter
½ cup raw sugar
1½ cups self-raising flour
salt
½ cup milk
1 egg, beaten
2 tablespoons golden (corn) syrup or honey, plus extra to serve
cream, to serve

1   Grease a medium-sized pudding basin and arrange orange slices around the base
    and sides.

2   Cream together butter and sugar until light and fluffy. Stir in flour and salt to taste
    alternately with milk and egg, then beat until smooth. Stir in grated orange zest.

3   Warm golden (corn) syrup or honey and spoon over the base and sides of the
    orange-lined basin. Spoon in pudding mixture, cover basin tightly with foil and tie
    with string, forming a loop at the top so that the basin may be easily removed from
    the slow cooker.

4   Place basin in slow cooker. Boil 2–4 cups water and pour into base of cooker, then
    cook on high for approximately 5 hours. Carefully remove the pudding basin and turn
    pudding out. Slice the pudding and serve with a little extra warmed golden syrup or
    honey spooned over each slice, topped with a dab of cream.

Fruity-Favourite
Steamed Pudding

Preparation time: 45 minutes
Cooking time: 5 hours
Serves: 6–8

90g (3oz) butter
1 cups caster (berry) sugar
2 cups plain (all-purpose) flour
1½ teaspoons baking powder
½ teaspoon mixed spice
½ teaspoon bicarbonate of soda (baking soda)
salt
½ cup milk
1 egg
1 tablespoon raisins
1 tablespoon sultanas (golden raisins)
1 tablespoon dried dates, chopped
1 tablespoon dried apricots, chopped
1 tablespoon walnuts, chopped
hot custard, to serve

1 Grease a medium-sized pudding basin with a little of the butter. Cream the remainder with caster (berry) sugar in a separate basin, until light and soft.

2 Stir flour and baking powder together with mixed spice, bicarbonate of soda (baking soda) and salt to taste. Beat milk and egg together. Stir small quantities of sifted flour and beaten milk alternately into creamed butter mixture. Fold together lightly.

3 Stir in dried fruits and walnuts, and spoon mixture into basin. Cover tightly with foil and tie with kitchen string, forming a loop at the top so that the basin may be easily removed from the slow cooker.

4 Place basin in slow cooker and pour enough boiling water around the base to come halfway up the sides. Cook on high for approximately 5 hours. Turn out pudding onto heated serving platter and serve with hot custard.

Hot Caramel Meringue Pudding

Preparation time: 50 minutes
Cooking time: 2½–3½ hours
Serves: 4–6

¼ cup raw sugar
1½ cups evaporated milk
1 teaspoon vanilla extract
3 thick slices wholemeal (whole wheat) bread, crusts removed, cubed
⅓ cup sultanas (golden raisins)
⅓ cup raisins, chopped
zest of 1 orange, grated
3 eggs, separated
¼ cup unthickened (whipping) cream
1 teaspoon lemon juice
⅓ cup caster (berry) sugar
1 teaspoon dried coconut

1   Place raw sugar in a heavy-based saucepan and heat over low temperature, stirring gently until sugar has dissolved. Once melted, increase heat and allow to cook without stirring until a deep golden brown. Remove from heat.

2   Meanwhile, bring the milk to the boil. Pour boiling milk into the toffee gradually, stirring or whisking constantly to form a smooth caramel. Add vanilla.

3   Mix together bread cubes, dried fruits and orange zest. Add caramel and allow to stand for about half an hour.

4   Beat egg yolks and cream, and add lemon juice. Stir gently into cooling caramel mixture. Allow to become cold, then pour into an ovenproof basin, cover with foil and tie firmly with kitchen string. Fill the slow cooker with about 5cm (2in) of water and put in the basin. Cook on low for 2½–3 hours. Remove pudding basin, take off foil covering and allow to cool.

5   Preheat the oven to 200°C (400°F). Whip the egg whites, gradually adding the caster (berry) sugar, then swirl meringue onto top of cooled pudding and sprinkle with coconut. Place in oven and cook for 15–20 minutes or until meringue is golden brown and crisp.

Weights & Measures

Although recipes have been tested using the Australian Standard 250ml cup, 20ml tablespoon and 5ml teaspoon, they will work just as well with the US and Canadian 8fl oz cup, or the UK 300ml cup. We have used graduated cup measures in preference to tablespoon measures so that proportions are always the same. Where tablespoon measures have been given, they are not crucial measures, so using the smaller tablespoon of the US or UK will not affect the recipe's success. But we all agree on the teaspoon size.

For breads, cakes and pastries, the only area which might cause concern is where eggs are used, as proportions will then vary. If working with a 250ml or 300ml cup, use large eggs (65g/2¼oz), adding a little more liquid to the recipe for 300ml cup measures if it seems necessary. Use medium-sized eggs (55g/2oz) with an 8fl oz cup measure. A graduated set of measuring cups and spoons is recommended, the cups in particular for measuring dry ingredients. Remember to level such ingredients to ensure an accurate quantity.

Oven Temperatures

The Celsius temperatures given here are not exact; they have been rounded off and are given as a guide only. Follow the manufacturer's temperature guide, relating it to oven description given in the recipe. Remember gas ovens are hottest at the top, electric ovens at the bottom and convection-fan forced ovens are usually even throughout. We've included Regulo numbers for gas cookers, which may assist. To convert °C to °F multiply °C by 9 and divide by 5 then add 32.

	C°	F°	Gas Regulo
Very slow	120	250	1
Slow	150	300	2
Moderately slow	160	320	3
Moderate	180	350	4
Moderately hot	190–200	370–400	5–6
Hot	210–220	410–440	6–7
Very hot	230	450	8
Super hot	250–290	475–500	9–10

English Measures

English measurements are similar to Australian with two exceptions: the English cup measures 300ml/10½fl oz, whereas the American and Australian cups measure 250ml/8¾fl oz. The English tablespoon (the Australian dessertspoon) measures 14.8ml/½fl oz against the Australian tablespoon of 20ml/¾fl oz. The Imperial measurement is 20fl oz to the pint, 40fl oz a quart and 160fl oz per gallon.

American Measures

The American reputed pint is 16fl oz, a quart is equal to 32fl oz and the American gallon, 128fl oz. The American tablespoon is equal to 14.8ml/½fl oz, the teaspoon is 5ml/⅙fl oz. The cup measure is 250ml/8¾fl oz.

Dry Measures

All the measures are level, so when you have filled a cup or spoon, level it off with the edge of a knife. The scale opposite is the 'cook's equivalent'; it is not an exact conversion of metric to imperial measurement. To calculate the exact metric equivalent yourself, multiply ounces by 28.349523 to obtain grams, or divide grams by 28.349523 to obtain ounces.

Metric grams (g), kilograms (kg)	Imperial ounces (oz), pound (lb)	Metric grams (g), kilograms (kg)	Imperial ounces (oz), pound (lb)
15g	$\frac{1}{2}$oz	225g	8oz/$\frac{1}{2}$lb
20g	$\frac{2}{3}$oz	315g	11oz
30g	1oz	340g	12oz/$\frac{3}{4}$lb
55g	2oz	370g	13oz
85g	3oz	400g	14oz
115g	4oz/$\frac{1}{4}$lb	425g	15oz
125g	4$\frac{1}{2}$oz	455g	16oz/1lb
140/145g	5oz	1000g/1kg	35.3oz/2$\frac{1}{3}$lb
170g	6oz	1$\frac{1}{2}$kg	3$\frac{1}{3}$lb
200g	7oz		

Caster (berry) sugar is also known as superfine sugar.

Liquid Measures

Metric millilitres (ml)	Imperial fluid ounce (fl oz)	Cup and Spoon
5ml	$\frac{1}{6}$fl oz	1 teaspoon
20ml	$\frac{2}{3}$fl oz	1 tablespoon
30ml	1fl oz	1 tbsp + 2 tsp
55ml	2fl oz	
63ml	2$\frac{1}{4}$fl oz	$\frac{1}{4}$ cup
85ml	3fl oz	
115ml	4fl oz	
125ml	4$\frac{1}{2}$fl oz	$\frac{1}{2}$ cup
150ml	5$\frac{1}{4}$fl oz	
188ml	6$\frac{2}{3}$fl oz	$\frac{3}{4}$ cup
225ml	8fl oz	
250ml	8$\frac{1}{2}$fl oz	1 cup
300ml	10$\frac{1}{2}$fl oz	
370ml	13fl oz	
400ml	14fl oz	
438ml	15$\frac{1}{2}$fl oz	1$\frac{3}{4}$ cups
455ml	16fl oz	
500ml	17$\frac{1}{2}$fl oz	2 cups
570ml	20fl oz	
1 litre	35$\frac{1}{3}$fl oz	4 cups

Index